Cancer, Courage and
Collateral Damage

Cancer, Courage and Collateral Damage

An inspiring story of resilience, hope and determination

Raymond J. Stecker

Library of Congress Control Number:		2012919303
ISBN:	Hardcover	978-1-4797-3339-2
	Softcover	978-1-4797-3338-5
	Ebook	978-1-4797-3340-8

This book was printed in the United States of America.

To order additional copies of this book, contact:
Xlibris Corporation
1-888-795-4274
www.Xlibris.com
Orders@Xlibris.com
119122

Contents

Dedicated to my wife, Candy
and my daughters Kelly and Hadley,
whom I love more than life itself

The author prior to treatment

Preface

I had read a number of books and articles about cancer during the time I went through my experience, but I never found anything that described what actually goes on behind the curtain in your mind and in your heart.

What are the thoughts and feelings one experiences during an odyssey like cancer and all that comes with it, and in fact, what is all that comes with it?

This is not a guidebook, rather a story of a journey through the unknown. During this whole ordeal, the range of emotions is extreme. I experienced everything, from fear, sadness, panic, weakness, depression, isolation, loneliness, guilt, anger, pain, and disbelief to more fear and, believe it or not, flat-out, gut-wrenching laughter.

I thought a lot about everything I had gone through and how it has affected me and others around me. I thought writing something down might help me accept the transformation from who I was BC (before cancer) and who I became AC (after cancer). It also occurred to me that getting some hands-on information out there might be helpful for others.

No two cancers are the same nor are the treatments for them, but I wanted to give anyone who reads this an idea of what really happens. What you are going through is reality for you, and that is the issue you have to deal with day in and day out. Those of you who are reading this are fortunate like me; there are many others who are not.

This is at a minimum, a personal chronicle of what I went through and how my wife, Candy, and our children handled it. It is as if I have lived two different lives in two different places. One of them needed to be uncovered, documented, and better understood.

Cancer, Courage and Collateral Damage

Candy and I followed the doctor into a conference room where he had a series of brain scans snapped onto multiple monitors against one wall. He pointed out the abnormalities and tried to explain them to us, but we had no comprehension of what he was saying or what we were seeing. We then followed him back to his office. The first thing he said was that he would like me to be admitted to the hospital on Tuesday and keep me under observation, and he would perform brain surgery on the following Monday. It was as if he said, "We'll play gin rummy on Tuesday, and then on Monday, we'll play chess." Was this for real? We didn't know what to say or what to think.

I met my wife, Candace Elizabeth Dillon, in the late fall of 1975, after returning from a "college term abroad" program in Florence, Italy. I had blond hair and a full dark beard. My heart was hers the first time I saw her and has been every day since. We had dated through college. I went to Union in upstate New York, and as I started my business career in the Boston area, she finished her last year at Skidmore College, where she had transferred two years earlier. A year later, my first attempt at "Will you marry me?" was unsuccessful. Then in a flash, I was promoted (I worked for Procter and Gamble at that time) and was relocated to Denver, Colorado. We were then on separate paths for a year or so. Then in February of 1981, we got engaged over the phone (me still in Denver and Candy in Boston). In April, a brief visit from her in Denver started off with a broken leg for me in a lacrosse game on the first day she arrived. Our wedding date was set for August of that year. I arrived three days before the wedding, and then our honeymoon consisted of driving an old family station wagon with a U-Haul trailer attached to the bumper across country back to Denver. It was an adventurous trip. At one point, we stopped in Indiana to get gas. As I walked around the back of the car I noticed that the two clamps holding the U-Haul trailer to the old station wagon were just about to fall off the bumper. I was relieved, then suddenly panicked when the gas station attendant said he could not help since all of the mechanics were done for the day since it was after 5 o'clock. He said he could not help but that it would not be a problem since we were only a two miles from the time zone change and it was just 4:40 p.m. since we were very close to the border of Illinois and the gas station down the street would be able to help us! Candy and I started laughing at our good fortune. I married not only the woman of my dreams but the youngest in a family of four girls and took her more than halfway across the country. That took a lot of courage on her part. My eyes light up whenever she is in my sight, and they always will. Without her, I would only be half a person, and I know she feels the same way. Life is a roller coaster, and Candy is the only one I would ever want next to me on that lifetime ride. I am truly blessed.

We knew that we would eventually move back to New England to raise a family, which we did in 1984. I changed careers, took a 40 percent cut in pay, got started in the investment business, and settled in a suburb north of Boston named Beverly Farms.

For twelve years I commuted to Boston, most of the time by train, taking the 6:15 a.m. into the city or occasionally leaving very early in the morning by car with a friend (to beat the traffic) and taking the 9:00 p.m. train home.

In the summer, Candy would meet me at the train station with our first child (born in 1986) in a stroller and hand me a beer, and we would walk the short quarter-mile distance to our house. In 1990, our second daughter was born, and that same summertime routine was working well.

In the fall of 1999, my two daughters were about to enter the fourth and eighth grades and were at the same school, which was just a couple of miles from our home.

Then I took advantage of an opportunity to relocate my business up to the North Shore, about four miles from our house. Everything seemed great. I was working hard, yet the newfound balance in my life was providing me with the happiness and a lifestyle I had only dreamed was possible. I was enjoying the opportunity to be the best father I could be for my two girls and being involved in their lives and in the local community. For ten years, I was Uncle Sam in the Fourth of July parade and ran the children's races on the beach.

My own father had died when I was thirteen, and I wanted to be involved as much as I could with my children. I did not want them to miss what I missed. Candy and I talk about how those were some of the best times in our lives. We traveled with the children, creating memories for them and us as we journeyed through England, France, and other destinations. They were learning about history and different cultures and that the "old" house where we lived in Massachusetts was actually "new" compared to the thousand-plus-year-old places we visited abroad.

Back home, they learned to water ski, snow ski, play lacrosse, play tennis, scuba dive, as well as play sports at school. As for me, I worked out at the gym, logged many miles on early-morning weekend bike rides with a group of obsessed cyclists, and swam a mile in an outdoor pool (seventy-two lengths, with the first two underwater) a couple of times a week. I was in the best shape I had been in since college. I played a lot of golf and even won a couple of tournaments (with a partner, of course).

Life was good. My business was growing. My family was happy and healthy, and so was I. I was always a person who liked to do or try to do what people said I could not. Or do things they didn't think of or things they just plain wouldn't do. This was effective in sports and, even to some degree, later in the business world—the whole idea of thinking outside the box and being more determined than anyone else.

I was always optimistic, even in times when it might not make sense to be. I believed in myself, and above all, I never, ever gave up even when things looked bleak.

In college, when we were about to play a team that was acknowledged to be far superior to us, my attitude was "I don't care what your record is or what other teams you have beaten or what your stats are. Beat me today, beat us today." In golf, if I am playing someone who is a 3 handicap and I am a 7 (used to be), I do not want any strokes: beat me today, straight up. You know what, you will win once in a while, and it feels really, really good, and it is the same with life.

I do not know why I am like this. Maybe I am just wired this way, but it sure does help when trouble comes along. One of my favorite books when I was little was *The Little Engine That Could*. I do not know how many times that book was read to me or how many times I read it by myself, but I still think about that story a lot. My children got a very heavy dose of that book read to them.

Chapter 1

Something Doesn't Seem Right

One day in the late fall of 2000, I was doing sit-ups in the gym, and something seemed strange. I was getting a little dizzy. I rested for a few minutes and tried some more. This time the whole gym appeared to be moving, so I stopped. My initial thought was that I had a head cold of some sort. I lifted a few weights, didn't feel anything awkward, showered, and went on with my day. A week or so later, we took our children to the Topsfield Fair. This is one of the largest and oldest agricultural and carnival-type events on the Eastern Seaboard. There are many rides that a sane person or anyone over forty should just not go on. My children were able to convince me to go on the Egyptian Ship. This ride appeared to be very tame, just a pendulum like motion gradually increasing in height as it flowed from one side to the other.

I thought I had a head cold and was still wary of my stability, so just to be safe, I sat at one end near the bow so that I would have something to hold on to if I needed to. I felt a little wimpy for doing this, but I wanted to participate with my family. It turned out that I scared myself to death. The inside of my head spun so much that I didn't know if I could stay on. I was afraid of falling off this thing from eighty feet in the air. I kept telling myself to pretend that this was a war, and my life depended on holding on as hard as I could and to wait it out—it was that serious. Every time we came to level and then swung back up, I gripped on where I could, hoping that this would stop, but it didn't. I was determined to hang on as long as it lasted even if they had to pry my hands off at the end. I didn't know whether I should shut my eyes or keep them open—neither way improved anything. Finally it ended. I had never been more scared in my life than I was on this children's ride at a country fair on a lovely fall day in New England.

I thought I would die right there, either from falling off and getting flung who knows where or from a heart attack. After a couple of minutes on the ground, the nightmare dissipated. I did not share this with Candy other than say, "That really felt weird," and I did not say a word about it to my two girls.

A little later in the fall, my family and I went for a walk with our dog on the golf course. About one hundred yards or so off the first tee, there is an inclined slope, which is a perfect spot to roll down like a lot of us did as children. Again, I thought I would show my children that I could still mix it up with them.

That was a mistake! The inner horror I felt was even worse than on the Egyptian Ship. I felt as if I were falling off the edge of the earth. I had no idea if I was upside down or backward, horizontal or vertical. I had to wait awhile before I could stand up, and even then, I was still very disoriented.

Candy looked at me, and I looked at her. We both knew I had to see a doctor.

Chapter 2

Ear Infection

The next day, I called my primary care physician for an appointment and was able to get one for a couple of days later. There are some very excellent PCPs out there. Unfortunately, I did not have one of them at that time. I told him my story, and he looked down my throat, checked my blood pressure. He said it could be a brain tumor, but it was probably just a head cold or an inner ear infection and gave me a prescription for Mezzacline and said I should be fine in a few days. After five days with no improvement, I was starting to get a little frustrated, so I gave him a call. It was early January 2001. I told him that the medication was not working and that I needed to see a neurologist. So, without much enthusiasm, he gave me a referral to someone that I had heard was very good along with the number to call. I called the office of the neurologist who I had heard was very good. It was early January, and that office informed me that the earliest appointment was in April—four months away. I was annoyed and concerned about the delay, so I called my PCP again. He insisted that Dr. Smith was the best guy around and I should wait until then. I was beginning to get *really* frustrated.

I told him I could not wait until April and he had to find me a neurologist immediately. Two days later, he gave me a second referral, and I set up an appointment for two weeks later.

Chapter 3

Getting to Christopher Lloyd

You might remember the movie *Back to the Future* and the mad scientist played by actor Christopher Lloyd. Well, my neurologist was a man who reminded me of him.

Apparently, his main office was located in a suburb of Boston, but he had a satellite space in a small town nearby where I was scheduled to meet him. It was in a quaint-looking New England office park with an assortment of small businesses ranging from a dentist to an actuarial firm to a construction company.

As I entered, I could see a small reception area with a few chairs, which seemed the logical place to check in. I told the receptionist I was there to see Dr. Mark. She promptly told me she didn't work for him, giggled with a coworker, and told me to wait. It was a very awkward situation, and I felt like an idiot for going there. It was obvious he wasn't part of that group of doctors. The feeling was that they were putting up with this guy to collect some rent and had stuffed him in an area where they wouldn't have to be bothered by him and hoped none of their patients could see him. I was thinking maybe they knew something I didn't and that I should get out of there, but it was too late. I saw him walking down the hallway toward me with a somewhat awkward gait and white curly hair.

I followed him back to his very small office still unsure that I was doing the right thing or in the right place.

So I was in this little office. I sat on a table that took up most of the space, and I told him my symptoms. He went through the normal temperature, blood pressure, listen-to-your-heart drill. There was no assistant or nurse—they wouldn't have fit.

He had me lie on my back looking up at the ceiling. Then he suddenly put his hand behind my head, jerked my head up, and started twisting it from side to side while staring directly into my eyes. It was the most aggressive exam I had ever experienced. I thought he was either trying to hypnotize me or else had watched a few too many WWF matches. I didn't know whether to thank him or smack him one.

Was this why they had snickered at me in the lobby? He then said that I needed to get an MRI. All of a sudden, I loved this guy! He scheduled an MRI appointment to take place in two days and said he would get back to me with the results a day or two after that.

I walked out of there feeling really upbeat that my persistence had paid off and that I was on the path to finding out what was the cause of my dizziness. I was also glad I didn't lose my patience with him—I was close though!

Two days after my MRI, I receive a call from him saying that I needed to come back to his office. I asked if I had to come right away (my way of asking, "Is this serious?"). He said, "No, but could you make it there tomorrow afternoon?"

I said sure and was somewhat relieved until he replied, "You should also bring your wife." I wasn't sure what to think.

So the next day, Candy and I went to his "office." I had warned her of his eclectic appearance and nature. We sat down, well, one of us did (remember size-challenged office), and he said that he had shown my MRI slides to the entire neurology department of Beverly Hospital, and no one had ever seen anything like it before. He said I had to get to either Johns Hopkins, where he had contacts, or to Massachusetts General Hospital (MGH) right away. Well, he just confirmed what I already knew, that I was different than the "average bear" as stated by a character on the TV program *Rocky and Bullwinkle*. I watched it a lot when I was little, right along with *The Road Runner* and *The Three Stooges*: resilient characters all. I knew I would learn something from those shows! Little did I know then what the advantage of being "different" would mean in my future treatment.

Well, did I *dare* call my suboptimal primary care physician? Yes, as quickly as I could and for two reasons. First, to get referrals to see the top doctors for whatever it was that I had and, second, because now I had some leverage, and he was going to want to get me out of his life—fine with me.

I was able to get an appointment at Massachusetts General Hospital within the week. At this point, Candy was a little concerned, as any spouse would be. My inner optimistic wiring kicked into gear, and I told her not to worry until we actually had something to worry about. Also, except when doing sit-ups, going on carnival rides, or rolling down hills like a ten-year-old, I felt fine.

Chapter 4

Hello, Massachusetts Hospital

Candy and I drove forty minutes down Route 128 to Route 1 and onto Storrow Drive to Massachusetts General Hospital, known as Boston's largest teaching hospital.

We didn't know then that this same trip would be repeated thirty-seven times over the course of the next six months, plus over twenty times by Candy alone subsequent to that.

It was my first time in this institution, and it wasn't as I had expected. Walking in the main entrance, I felt like I was in a Star Wars movie. I have traveled a lot over the years, and my surprise was not the varying ethnicities or different languages but the different kinds of garb and many states of physical disrepair. I could not discern the doctors from the patients. Did the various hospital fashions signify different illnesses? Which people were contagious, and which were not? Some people wore masks over their mouths. Should I be wearing one? Where do I get one? Some were in scrubs, some in business attire with a stethoscope around their neck. Which people had the flu, which ones had a broken finger, and which ones did not have much longer to live? Some people certainly seemed to be in the latter category, but there was no discrimination. The desperate, feeble, and helpless looking were of all ages, races, and gender. Which would I be? Certainly none of them, I hoped (I kept those thoughts to myself). The most disturbing were the children—the ones in wheelchairs or with no hair or wearing a cap. Every time I saw a young child, I hoped that they had a severe case of diaper rash or just the flu or were visiting a grandparent. There was just no way of knowing.

The oddest thing was that everyone was walking around, seeming to me to be oblivious to their surroundings. How could they all walk around as if this was all normal? People die in this place; many peoples' lives change forever in this place and frequently not for the better. It's like a mass of worker ants moving and bumping along, some at warp speed, some at super slow speed, changing lanes and direction indiscriminately for the most part without running into one another. Some were stable, and some were not. Some needed assistance; others needed a lot of assistance. *I do not really have to be here, do I?*

It didn't feel right. I had my khakis, white shirt, tie, and blue blazer on—I looked normal. I felt like I was cheating and getting looks as if all the minds moving around were saying, "What are you doing here? You don't belong here. Let us deal with our misery. Don't flaunt your healthy status around us."

I did not express any of this to Candy. I was totally focused on getting to the doctor we needed to see as soon as possible so he could tell us that there was nothing seriously wrong with me. Then we could leave and never come back.

Candy and I found our way to the sixth floor and the Brain Tumor Center, indicated by a little sign on the wall next to the door. Just walking into a room with that title was a very strange feeling. If I had been going into that environment to visit a friend, it would have been strange enough, but going there as a potential patient was eerie.

For some reason, I had this picture in my mind of a high-tech office with lots of space, prints on the wall, and nicely arranged office furniture. But staff desks were all close by and contiguous to the waiting area. From what I could see, this place needed a serious upgrade. So right off the bat, this did not instill a lot of confidence, which really didn't matter to me at that time because I *knew* I didn't need to be there. Part of me felt we were many levels higher up on the medical food chain than we needed to be because we had forced the issue. The other side of me felt that there might be something wrong, but being there would verify that my issues were, in fact, minor. If we ended up killing an ant with a sledge hammer, so be it. At least we would know it won't be coming back.

The immediate staff and the waiting area were in a fairly small space. I was hoping that not too many people would come in after us because they might not fit.

Candy started reading very intensely brain tumor and cancer material that she had picked up from a stack of pamphlets that were situated in a rack on the wall next to her. I could tell that she was trying to find out everything she could. On the other hand, I was quite casual since I "knew" nothing was seriously wrong with me, plus if I also jumped on the reading material (even out of curiosity), she would take it as a sign that I was worried, and thinking that I was worried would make her worry even more. It's funny how simple things can ratchet up the emotional levels in a hurry. I did not want to add anything to the concerns that might be going through Candy's mind.

Candy asked to use the ladies' room, which under most circumstances would not be an unusual request. The nice woman at the desk pointed to a door a few feet away, then cautioned Candy to be careful—the toilet was hot. Candy, as polite as always, said, "Excuse me, you mean the room is hot?"

As Candy got up, the woman said, "No, the toilet water is hot."

Candy started laughing, saying, "You're joking, right?" Again, no was the reply. Candy went in and closed the door. We could all hear her laughing behind the door. When she came out, Candy was crying. She was laughing so hard and almost fell to the ground. She asked why the water was so hot that steam was coming from the toilet bowl. The woman said she didn't know and it was crazy and that someone was coming to fix it.

She was laughing too while taking it right in stride. I couldn't believe it and went over to confirm for myself and decided if that toilet water was that close to boiling, God only knows what else was going on in those pipes, and if I had to use the bathroom, I was going to find another location. Once again, this little episode didn't really do much to reassure me that we were headed in the right direction. I felt for a moment that Allen Funt, the guy who hosted *Candid Camera* in the '60s and '70s, would jump out from behind some curtain and say, "Smile! You're on *Candid Camera*." The quasi-comedy show took our minds off the myriad thoughts of what might come next.

Chapter 5

Am I Really Talking to a Brain Surgeon?

As the doctor appeared, I felt an instant feeling of connection and comfort level. He had a warm, genuine, and caring way about himself. His whole demeanor exuded quiet expertise as though he had been through this a thousand times. It was as if he were saying, "Don't worry, things are going to be all right. I will take care of you."

We summarized the brief history of how we ended up in his office. He then took us into a large conference room and brought us over to a wall with multiple high-tech screens showing multiple views of the inside of someone's brain. My brain.

His manner had a soft touch and expert knowledge that came across in a natural, tender, and caring way. This wasn't putting on a show for us; this was really him. We could tell that he cared but had no idea that what he was about to tell us would change our lives forever. He pointed out various areas of my brain and their varying functions. Then came the area of concern.

There was some sort of tumor, about the size of a small orange, located in the back of my head, in the cerebellum. It was very interesting to see and hear his description of all of this, but it was like hieroglyphics to me. There was no air of him being condescending or patronizing to us. He made us feel like he was talking to equals even though he must have been dumbing it down somewhat, but you would never know. He was direct with his eye contact and gracious in his manner. I will just never forget it. From that moment on, I trusted him completely and without reservation.

Chapter 6

You Are Going to Do What?

We followed him back to his office, and he sat down in front of his computer. He did not appear to be alarmed. He simply said he would like me to come in as an inpatient on Wednesday and be operated on the following Monday. Was this for real? I didn't know what to say or what to think. What was I supposed to say? "Gee, let me think about it," or "Let me check my calendar." If one of the best brain surgeons in one of the best hospitals in the country asks me to come in on Wednesday to have an opportunity to save my life, I think I just might be able to make it! He said it was possible this could be cancer, but I was still approaching this from the standpoint that there was something in my head that needed to come out—I wasn't thinking that I had cancer.

I was in very good physical shape (just ask Candy), and I felt too strong (ask Candy again) for this to be anything serious. But I did ask him if we could step back for a minute and if he could walk us through one more time.

I was able to absorb more on the second telling, especially when it came to my two treatment options. One was to do a resection (take the tumor out). But because my tumor hadn't responded to contrast dye, there was a 35 percent chance of not being able to walk again. One aspect of the uniqueness of my situation was the "not responding to contrast dye" issue. As it turns out, the lack of response of the brain cells to the dye means that the surgeons cannot determine where the tumor (whether benign or malignant) begins or ends. Hence, the higher the risk of removing good cells along with the bad. It's like flying blind. So if I am going to be on a plane with those guys, I prefer them to have their eyes open.

The second option was to do an open biopsy, quite a procedure in itself, but at least I wouldn't have to deal with the wheelchair issue right away. My position quickly became "If I am going to be six feet under in six months, I'll go for the first option, but if we can wait, I'd rather pursue the second option." He agreed, thank God. I now knew my negotiating skills were getting better!

On the way back home, Candy and I had plenty to talk about. I kept reinforcing my true belief that they were going to go in there and find the tumor, or whatever it was, and get out the turkey baster and just suck that thing out of there. End of story. There was no way it could be anything else.

It couldn't be anything else because we have two children. Two beautiful, wonderful girls—fourteen and ten years old at that time and at the same school, in the fourth and eighth grades.

We had not discussed anything with the children since I had only been to doctor visits while they were at school. We did not want to alarm them unnecessarily. However, I was going to be in the hospital for a few days; we had to say something. Now we did not know what I had or what was going to happen or if this was a quick fix or not. So we told the children that I was going into the hospital for some evaluation and that if there was anything to worry about, we would let them know right away. In the meantime, there was no need to be concerned and "just go about your days as usual." That worked fine. Candy and I were taking the same approach.

I was scheduled to be admitted to the MGH on February 21 and to be operated on February 28. Some close friends had invited us on a short ski weekend with their children on President's Day weekend, arriving in Vermont in the late afternoon of the seventeenth and returning on the nineteenth. Candy and I discussed whether we should go on this trip given the circumstances. We ended up thinking that the children were looking forward to it and a little respite before our upcoming ordeal might be a good thing.

As an aside, I had learned to ski as a child on the icy slopes of New England and later spent some time working in Denver, Colorado, and had the opportunity to ski the powder-filled slopes of Vail. What a wonderful experience and a completely different sensation than East Coast skiing. Candy was an accomplished skier in her own right.

We had a nice dinner Friday night, and everyone was looking forward to getting on the slopes the next morning. I do not know why I thought I would be able to ski. I guess I thought that since these first few runs would be over modest terrain, there would not be a problem. I guessed wrong.

After about fifty feet, I realized that just getting down the slope would be a Herculean task. I had no feeling in my legs. The surgeon and I did not have a conversation in regard to attempting any significant physical activity, and this total ineptitude took me by surprise. I thought about having the ski patrol take me down but realized that would mean everyone would know something was wrong. So I stayed in back "in case any of the children fell and needed help." I was finally able to make it down by reverting to a small child's "snow plow" technique.

No one seemed to notice except Candy. I feigned a sore back, and Candy gave me a ride to our guesthouse nearby. We had another nice dinner, played board games with the children, and retired for the night. The next day, I stayed at the house reading some and going through all sorts of scenarios in my mind—most of them somber and morbid. I was fearful of what lay ahead. We left Sunday morning and made it back home without incident and with our secret intact. I did not think it was appropriate to tell our hosts that I might have cancer. It would have put a damper on the weekend, and I wanted everyone to have a good time, particularly the children of both families.

Candy and I had the time between that Monday and the upcoming Thursday to discuss various issues that were quickly approaching: What would happen after the operation? Would Candy be able to see me beforehand? Would she be there afterward? And many more questions that we couldn't even fathom.

If possible, I wanted to end up in a private hospital room. Although I had had no experience in this area, I suspected that after having my skull cut open, I wouldn't be in the mood to chat it up with anyone. Plus I wasn't going to be sympathetic to someone else's problems, and I did not want to hear anyone else's moaning and groaning as I was going to have a tough enough time on my own. As it turned out, I was able to get a private room—great, one less thing to worry about.

Maybe in these serious surgery cases, this was standard procedure. I didn't know, but it was fine with me. Again, I thought I was going to be out of there shortly after my lobotomy (only kidding), but I'd rather be safe than sorry. I didn't want someone upchucking or crying in pain in the bed next to me to add to my own misery.

> Another sidebar. Candy, by nature, is a very kind, genuine, and caring person. She has been trying for over thirty-four years to help me morph my persona to adopt just a little more of those qualities. I truly believe I possess those attributes, but they are not always as readily apparent. Truth be told, I wish I could be more like her, and she wishes she could be a very, very, very little bit like me. Maybe that is one reason our marriage is so strong.

On Wednesday morning of the twenty-first, we headed to Boston and the MGH. We went to the room, which was quite nice actually. Candy had brought some flowers and pictures of the children to make everything look homier. She wanted the doctors and nurses to know I had a family who loved me and to take good care of me for my two little precious daughters. She even brought new pajamas for me so that when the time came, I would feel more comfortable than wearing the traditional backless gown, which seems to be the outfit du jour of any hospital I have ever been in. She thought the doctors would linger more in the room if it was sunny, clean, cheerful and if it smelled better. Candy had to leave in the afternoon to pick up the girls at school. I had a couple of books and some business magazines, so I was all set.

Later that day, a young doctor came in who was working with the surgeon on my case. She did some blood work and other minor tests. After a couple of hours, she returned to tell me that my blood work wasn't quite what it should be and that I had to return home until I heard from them.

I was surprised and a little disappointed. I was all geared up and ready to go. I was in the flow of the mo, as they say, emotionally, mentally, and physically. To have that interrupted was a bit of a downer, but at least the next time I came in, we would know where we were going and how to get there. The next day at the office, I got a call from my new friend, the brain surgeon. He asked me where I had gone as he had looked for me in my hospital room. He said that he went up to my room to see me and I wasn't there. I said that his assistant told me to go home because my Coumadin levels were too high.

Coumadin is a blood thinner I was on since a few years ago when I was diagnosed with an irregular heartbeat. As a result, you have to stop taking it five days before any procedure as it might cause bleeding; if you don't, you may have a problem stopping any bleeding.

> This was just another of my health "isms," which kicked in after knee surgery about ten years earlier. At that time, Candy had come to visit when I was in post op. There were a lot of wires attached to me; she saw them, and then she fainted, very gracefully, I was told. The reason Candy fainted was that after the operation, the orthopedic surgeon said that I had a heart problem during the procedure. She told him that my father had died of a heart attack at the age of fifty-seven. The surgeon's face turned white, and he immediately ran to get the cardiologist. I was still unconscious when I yelled out, "I shanked it." The nurses and Candy jumped up a mile. The nurses thought I had screamed out some sort of profanity. Candy explained that it was a golf term for an inferior shot. Later that day, I had to be cardioverted. She did not see my body pop up like you see on TV, but she was brought in immediately afterward. Later, when Candy told me the story, we laughed hysterically, thankful that I had not screamed out some insulting expletive during this unconscious state.

I wasn't too sure how an irregular heartbeat (technically atrial fibrillation) and brain surgery got along. I suspected not well, but I tried to forget about it.

The surgeon said that he knew the blood work would be off but wanted to keep me under observation. He said to come back tomorrow. I could tell he wasn't happy with the situation, and I liked that because it meant he was looking after me. I was gaining more and more confidence in him. Candy and I went back the next day. I was able to get the same room, and Candy had brought flowers and a plant and some family pictures from home. Candy is so good at these things. She said she wanted the doctor and others attending me to know I had a family who loved me and needed me and that I was worth saving. Also, she wanted the room to look good so they wouldn't just rush in, then rush out of the room quickly. She rearranged what little furniture there was, and it actually looked nice. Eventually, the surgeon would come in, sit on the small couch, and listen to us tell stories about our children in the pictures. We got to know him, and he got to know us. Candy came to visit almost every day, looking terrific; it really lifted my spirits as I began thinking of what was to come. I couldn't believe I was actually going to have *brain surgery*! When I was younger, brain surgery had been a recurring joke—as in "It's not brain surgery."

Now it didn't seem so funny.

On the last day before the "big dig," the surgeon came to the room in the early afternoon and sat down with us. He was very calm and reassuring. He went through the procedure step by step and asked if we had any questions. But what was I going to ask? What kind of drill bit was he going to use? Did it come from Home Depot?

That did not seem appropriate. I did ask, "What time of day are you at your best?" To which he replied, "I am always at my best." He wasn't cocky, but he was good at his job and wasn't afraid to say so. I knew the right guy was in charge. He then said, "Things will be fine," and he reminded me this wasn't a resection, just an open biopsy to determine if the tumor was cancerous and what kind. Translation: boring through my very thick skull and into my brain with some heavy-duty power tools.

For the uninitiated, many biopsies simply involve the insertion of a needle to collect some tissue as a sample. So the comparison might be akin to the difference between getting your teeth cleaned versus getting a root canal and your wisdom teeth pulled out at the same time. In my case, the tissue is in my brain, hence the need to go through the skull, resulting in a more complex and invasive procedure.

He said I would be out and would not feel anything and told Candy where the room was for people waiting for the doctors who would be coming out of surgery to update families on the status of their loved one's operation. Then he gave us the timeline—ten in the next morning. I could see Candy's eyes welling up with tears. I reassured her. I said, "I will be fine, I promise."

She asked back, "You promise?"

And I said, "Yes, I promise." Then to myself, "I *can* do this and I *will* do this. I will be fine, I promise!" After a kiss and a long, strong hug, she left for the evening drive home.

Then I did ask the surgeon one question that had been bothering me. Would he hide the Black and Decker power tools? I knew I would feel better if I didn't have to see them right before we got started. He said, "Don't worry, I will cover them up for you." I thanked him, and we smiled at each other as he walked out of the room.

That evening was tough. I was about to get my head sliced open like a grapefruit! Part of me couldn't believe this was happening; the other part of me almost felt like laughing. I was determined to not let this get the better of me. I knew I would get through it for Candy and the girls no matter what! But I also thought that this might be the last time I would ever be myself. How would I deal with a different Ray, and what would that mean to my family? I had always been invincible to my girls and to Candy (through our six years together before marriage and another nineteen years since). My biggest worry, however, was Candy. I did not know how she would be able to drive home from the hospital that day.

I could not imagine what would be going through her mind. I knew she would arrive at home and tell the kids that Daddy was doing fine and that she was going to see him again tomorrow.

Then she would cook dinner, jump into school topics with a smile on her face, right up until she went to our room and our bed to face the horror all by herself. Neither of us had any idea how many times that would be repeated over the next ten months. It saddens me to the depths of my heart and soul, even now.

Chapter 7

Abort Mission

As I was trying to get to sleep the night before my surgery (I didn't know how I was even going to be able to sleep), a nurse came into my room and handed me a cup with a couple of pills in it. I asked her what they were for, and she just stood there. She just stood there with a blank stare. Then it dawned on me:

"Dr. Chiocca wants me to take these, right?" A nod of the head was her silent reply. "He wants me to get a good night's sleep, right?"

This time the nod included a polite smile indicating that now I was beginning to understand. It made sense: he wouldn't want me to go through an anxious, fear-induced all-nighter right before the big event.

I woke the next morning after having slept like a rock. Of course, there was no breakfast. A little while later, two "materials management" attendants transferred me to a mobile bed, and before I knew it, I was on my way to the operating room.

I had never heard the term "materials management" before, but I became very familiar with it over the next few months. These are the people whose job it is to transfer paper, linen, food, beds, wheelchairs, canes, walkers, and other "material"—*people*—to their designated destination in a timely manner. They navigate the highways, back roads, and dark alleys of the MGH to perfection. To them, a ream of paper, a mattress, a bedpan, or a person, it's all the same—just get that piece of material to where it needs to go. You get pushed around with wires and tubes all over you and pass some doctors and also everyone else imaginable. Some people stare at you, and others ignore you. You are out there completely exposed in a feeble and weakened state, and you would prefer that absolutely no one sees you.

I thought the term was suboptimal. In my mind "patient transportation" was more accurate and a little more dignified, and anyone being shuffled around in this place needs more of that!

I could feel my heartbeat speeding up (this can't be good for someone who is A-fib and about to have brain surgery). Then it hit me: we were almost an hour ahead of time, and I haven't had a chance to see Candy.

I tried to tell them that they were bringing the wrong person down, as my surgery wasn't scheduled until 10:00 a.m. But they assured me they had it right: there had been an opening, and my doctor wanted to do the operation now. My heart was beating faster, and I was starting to feel that things were not right. How could I do this without seeing Candy? I could actually die in this sterile operating room in the basement of MGH without having had a chance to have a last kiss or last "I love you, I will come back to you" hug.

I was wheeled into an anteroom that opened into the operating room.

As I turned my head, I could see a lot of equipment that I had hoped would be out of sight. An anesthesiologist arrived and gave me an injection in my left arm and asked me to take off my wedding ring, but I told her that the ring has never been off my finger and that this was the last situation in which I would want to remove it. She kindly wrapped some tape around the ring and my finger. I then asked if this was going to put me out, and she said no and that it was just some Valium to help calm me down. I thanked her as I knew I seriously needed it. At this moment, I was as terrified as I had ever been both because of what was about to happen and because I might die without ever telling Candy how much I loved her, one last time.

But what happened next pushed me over the edge. All of a sudden, two nurses right behind me began arguing about one of their coworkers as if I wasn't even there. They were both getting worked up about some perceived slight. But there I was scared out of my mind. I haven't had a chance to see Candy, and I was about to get my skull and brain cut open and conceivably die. All while they were bickering like a couple of teenagers.

I couldn't take it anymore. I turned around the best I could and yelled, "Do YOU MIND?" One of them took a step back in an apologetic manner; the other one scurried up to me, held my left hand, and started to apologize profusely. My eyes filled with tears. She apologized some more, but it was just making me feel worse. Finally, I asked her to stop. I thought this might be a signal that I should back out of the procedure. It all felt so wrong, especially without seeing Candy.

Then the surgeon walked in. He asked how I was doing. I lied and said fine as I did not want his mind on anything but the task at hand. I asked why we were doing this earlier than scheduled. He said something opened up, and this was a good time to get it done. (I thought maybe someone had gone through what I had just gone through and had cancelled.)

He put me at ease though, and after all, he was the one who had to have his mind-set right, not me. At this point, I had been wheeled into the main operating room, and they were just about to dial up the anesthesia to put me out when the phone rang. I thought, *Now what?* The surgeon grabbed the phone and listened briefly. He hung up and told me that Candy had just arrived at the hospital, and he was going to wait.

I couldn't believe it! Tears still come into my eyes when I think of that moment. Candy arrived a few minutes later in full scrubs from head to toe escorted by a nurse attired in the same manner.

She leaned over and gave me a kiss and a hug as best as she could (given all the tubes and various contraptions I was attached to). That was exactly what I needed to get my courage and inner strength fired up. I was ready now. Plus she looked really cute in the surgery uni. She could have been a character on the TV series *ER*.

Chapter 8

Seven Hours Later

The surgeon was right: I didn't feel a thing. When I woke up, Candy was there. It was so good to see her. I was very groggy and uncomfortable, but not in any pain (morphine can do wonders). An attendant came in and said I had to stay completely still for the next five hours. I was positioned in a sitting up position on the bed since the six-inch incision in the back of my head had to be kept elevated. So here I was still uncomfortable and with orders not to move for five hours. I typically have trouble staying still for five minutes—never mind five hours. I watched every minute go by on the clock—it was pure torture. Then I felt something weird going on with my legs and realized that I had inflating wraparound cushions encompassing both legs, which compressed and released every few minutes. I learned this was to keep the blood flow going, assuming I still had enough to do so! Finally, a nurse came in and said I could "scooch" down a little bit. It is amazing sometimes how one little change can have such a big impact. I was more comfortable.

Before long, the surgeon came in, and I could tell he was in a good mood, which is why I wasn't prepared for what came next. He said I had cancer. The word just hung out there for a very long time, and I couldn't hold back the tears. But then he added the good part—that it wasn't the type of cancer he had feared, which would have been a death sentence. I wasn't sure how I would process this. Cancer terrified me. But I wasn't going to die, at least not right away, and it didn't look like I was going to need a wheelchair right away either.

That was enough for my psyche to shift into positive mode and prepare for whatever fight remained ahead even though I knew it wouldn't be easy. I looked at Candy with my determined "We are going to get through this" look to reassure her that I was going to make it. I wanted her to know I was confident and ready to do battle. A while later while I was still in intensive care, and a very large male attendant came into my room. I was still in half-sit-up position, and he said he was there to give me a sponge bath. I was not feeling too enthusiastic about this, but I was not in a position to object. It was fine, but just a little strange.

I am beginning to realize and understand at least one aspect about this whole patient thing in the hospital—you are just a product to be handled by them, so forget about any modicum of modesty because nobody cares except you.

Before I got out of intensive care, there was one other interesting experience. I was beginning to feel that I had to go to the bathroom, and I was thinking, *How are they going to have me do that since I am not permitted to move? I guess I will have to press the nurse call button to get a bedpan.* Then after a couple of minutes, my thought was, *Gee, I think I am going to the bathroom!* I picked up the bed sheet and saw that a catheter and been inserted. I laughed to myself. No one had told me that was part of the program, plus I had never had the experience before, so I did not know what was going on. A couple of days later, the catheter removal was done by a Simmons College coed, supervised by a nurse. By her hesitancy and the sudden flushed tone of her face, I could tell she was more uncomfortable than I was. I chuckled to myself.

Eventually, my materials management pals returned me to my room. I spent a few days under observation. Candy visited every day (always looking spectacular). The nurse phlebotomist took samples of my blood regularly (including all hours of the night). My vitals were taken by the regular nurses, and the surgeon visited a couple of times a day. Visits by Candy and the surgeon were the highlights of my day. Candy for obvious reasons and the surgeon because he was the one who was guiding me through this whole ordeal. And I had confidence in him and personally liked him.

After several days under observation, I had an appointment with the radiation oncologist on the lower level of the MGH.

Miraculously, I was able to walk, with some assistance, into a small office with Candy. We were seated and asked to wait. Within a few minutes, the radiation oncologist came in along with another doctor and introduced themselves. Following them, another six doctors paraded into the room. Except for Candy and me, it was standing room only. I thought to myself that this must be fairly serious if this many doctors were in there.

The radiation oncologist began to explain a procedure, called a "simulation", that I would go through the next day to prepare me for my eventual radiation protocol, which would start after I completed chemotherapy treatment.

I was very determined to beat this thing, and despite the surgery ordeal, I still had my optimism intact. In addition, I wanted the radiation oncologist to know that if he had to give me a bit of an overdose to kill whatever it was I had, to go ahead—I could take it. So I said, "Whatever you give everyone else, give me double." Without much of a pause, he replied, "Don't worry, we're going to hurt you." I immediately realized that he knew what was ahead much better than I did and that my sense of bravery was naive. In any event, I wanted him to know I did not want him to back off during the treatment process even if it meant tough times ahead for me. The goal was to kill the cancer!

As I learned later, this procedure is essentially a method of mapping your brain (and in my case, my spine as well) so that when the time comes for the radiation, you will set up to be "irradiated" in the proper locations for the appropriate amount of time. This simulation is done in advance in order to avoid any delays in my treatment transition from chemotherapy to radiation therapy.

The MM boys took me down the next day for my simulation. Afterward, I would be allowed to leave with Candy (somewhat like a work release program) for a day or so. Candy was with me, as she has been through just about everything.

The area for this procedure was in the lower level of the hospital, adjacent to other radiation treatment rooms. I ended up spending a lot of time down there in subsequent weeks. That first time, I was wheeled in and helped onto a table and given an explanation of what was going to happen. The attendants attached a special mask to my head and face to assist with the mapping procedure. My role was to lie on my stomach and stay absolutely still. It sounded simple enough, but I should have guessed it wouldn't be quite that easy. The mask, which was form fitted to my head and face, was analogous to chicken wire and molded so tightly against my face that I could not even blink my eyes. I took the instructions to lie face down and stay still very seriously since my life depended on it. I did not know how long this was going to take, and I am glad I didn't because for the next hour and twenty minutes, I didn't move an inch. The technicians offered words of encouragement along the way. But with the eventual nose dripping, mouth drooling, and the need to itch testing my resolve, I had to keep reminding myself that my life might depend on my staying as still as a statue even if spiders started crawling up my nose.

When it was all over, I was helped off the bed and felt a little woozy as the mask was removed from. As I started to leave the room, I looked in the mirror and could not believe what I saw. My face looked like an alien from another planet. A deep impression of the chicken wire was etched across my face! All of us—technicians, nurses, Candy, and I—laughed out loud. One of the technicians even took a picture.

Another comical part of this adventure occurred as we walked through the halls to leave the hospital after this procedure. I remembered the feeling of first entering the MGH. Well, the tide had turned. With every step I made, the seas parted as they did for Moses centuries ago. I could see the look in people's eyes as they stepped aside to allow my passage. I could imagine them thinking as they moved as far away from me as possible that they didn't want whatever it was that I had. I was laughing to myself at how much had changed in such a short time and how I had become one of the denizens of the Star Wars movie that I had pictured the first day I walked into the MGH.

The surgery was on February 28. From February 22 to March 2, I had four MRIs and one bone scan. In the days between the MRIs and the simulation, we met with our surgeon and neuro-oncologist to discuss getting a second opinion before starting down the treatment path. They agreed and gave us the names of three specialists: two in Maryland (one located at Johns Hopkins in Baltimore and the other at the National Cancer Institute in Bethesda) and the third (a renowned pathologist) located at the National Children's Medical Center in Washington, DC.

Also during this brief hiatus, we were able to handle a couple of personal issues, usually over lunch at the MGH cafeteria, which was one of the cafeterias I had ever eaten at. The basement of the hospital isn't the best location, but it was a lot better than what was getting dished out to me on the upper levels!

During one of these luncheon dates, we ran into a woman we know from the North Shore who apparently does volunteer work at the hospital. She was surprised to see me and asked why I was there. I told her that I had a little problem and turned my head to show her the six-inch stapled incision running down the back of my head. She almost fell to the floor. At that time, I looked absolutely normal from the front; it was only the view from behind that revealed anything askew.

Our girls' spring vacation was approaching in a few days, and we had planned to go south. However, our doctors advised us that traveling any significant distance would not be a good idea. I called Delta Air Lines and explained the situation and was told that I would need to go in person to the Delta ticket counter with a doctor's note. Luckily, there was a Delta office in Boston not far from the hospital.

Things did not proceed smoothly. Granted, there were only about ten days until our scheduled departure, but I did have a typewritten explanation on MGH-Brain Tumor Center stationary signed by a neurosurgeon and the chief of neuro-oncology. If that isn't the best teacher's note for not doing your homework, I do not know what is! As she looked up at me, I expected her to fall all over herself expressing her sympathy for what I was going through with a reply similar to "Oh, I am so sorry. Let me take care of that for you." Instead I heard, "This may not be sufficient, so I will have to make a phone call." I was about to come out with some choice remarks, but I held myself in check. So I turned and showed her the back of my head and asked, "Will this help?" I had my rebate vouchers in five minutes—no phone call needed.

Chapter 9

Road Trip

We met with our surgeon and neuro-oncologist to verify the three specialists they recommended we see for second opinions before I started treatment at MGH. I had the opportunity to take care of another issue.

I knew I would lose my hair as the result of my forthcoming treatment, so I went to my longtime barber and asked him to take a close blade to my hair. I wanted to eliminate my hair on my terms rather than passively have it happen to me while I was in a weakened state. Maybe this was a control issue, but I didn't know how much control I would have in the future, and I wanted to use what little I had left. I told my barber to take it all off and that this might be the last haircut he would be giving me for quite some time. Now, ten years out from my treatment, trimming the erratic remnants of hair I do have costs about as much as a Starbucks coffee. We both laugh about that!

Candy was, miraculously, able to schedule a flight to Baltimore/Washington Airport on short notice and also schedule three back-to-back appointments. There were some complications, however. Our appointment at Johns Hopkins in Baltimore and our appointment at the National Cancer Institute in Bethesda (an hour's drive away) were at the same time, 9:30 a.m., and there were no other options. We decided to take an earlier flight and arrive an hour early for our first meeting, hoping we could get in to see the first doctor and then hustle to the National Cancer Institute and try to make that appointment. We reasoned that we probably wouldn't get a second chance to see these specialists and hoped that the second doctor would take pity on us, even if we arrived late.

The third appointment was scheduled for the afternoon in Washington, DC, so that would not be a problem. Candy and I had made the decision before we left Boston that we did not want to take the risk of getting lost and missing our only opportunity to get these second opinions and that the money spent to have someone drive us who knew the area would be worth it. This was about saving my life, and I didn't want to take any unnecessary chances, so that was what we did—thank God.

Johns Hopkins

We were met at the airport and headed right for Johns Hopkins Hospital, which is not exactly in the best part of Baltimore. Right away, we knew that having a driver was money well spent. We arrived almost an hour early, and we were told to wait in the reception area.

After a few minutes, a man in a leather jacket walked in through the reception area without acknowledging our presence. I remember wondering who he was because he certainly didn't look like a cancer doctor.

After a little while, Dr. John Coen came out to greet us and apologized for not acknowledging us sooner. Since he wasn't expecting us so early, he assumed we were pharmaceutical salespeople. We did not want to offend him by telling him that we were early so that we could make the next appointment at the National Cancer Institute. I did not know if that would come across correctly. We had brought the most recent MRI scan with us, which turned out to be a big help. We did not want to rely on him having the capability to access to the scan electronically, which would have seemed likely, but we didn't want to take any chances. Can you imagine him saying, "Oh, I am sorry. I do not have access, and if you do not have them with you, I cannot offer an opinion"?

For a lot of things in life, but particularly in personal health issues, you have to be your own advocate even if it is in an area where you do not have any expertise. No one, no matter how accomplished they are in their profession or discipline, has as much vested interest in you as you do. No one knows your body as well as you do. You may not be able to diagnose what is wrong, but you know something is wrong. When that happens, do not procrastinate; take action. The best thing you can do is to be a good question asker. Be aware that professionals in areas of expertise outside of your own cannot help you or find solutions for you without good, honest questions from you and good honest answers to their questions. You have the ability to ask these questions even if you think you do not. A good professional will have the answer or be able to find the answer. So speak up!

After he finished examining me and looking at my MRI, he recommended doing radiation first. He asked if we were seeing anyone else, and we told him that we were headed to the National Cancer Institute. He commented they were good doctors over there and said he would write a report and send it to MGH.

National Cancer Institute

As we were on our way to the NCI we were already thankful for our session at Johns Hopkins as the doctor's recommendation was contrary to the scheduled protocol at Massachusetts General. We were very curious and anxious to hear from the oncologists at the NCI, but at the same time, I felt empowered that we were doing all we could.

During this whole nightmare, Candy and I were very scared. Part of that fear came from not knowing if we were doing all we could in terms of seeing every specialist and exploring every avenue. For me, each doctor we saw and each extra step we took reinforced that we were doing everything we could. Knowing this gave me the courage and strength to accept whatever happened. If we had been more passive, I don't know if I could have dealt with the uncertainty. I still had to beat cancer, but at least I had one less thing to worry about.

Of course we arrived late at the NCI due to our scheduling problem and just crossed our fingers that they would work us into the schedule.

As we walked into the reception area, I could see that the waiting area was packed, and I was prepared for a very long wait. We checked in, and almost before we sat down, Candy and I were called in to see the doctor. In the back of my mind, it occurred to me that maybe this immediate access was the result of the rarity of my illness and the challenge of figuring it out. I thought this type of unusual situation must really get them jazzed up—works for me!

We were escorted to the doctor's office, and within a couple of minutes, there was Dr. Howard Fine—young, in good shape, affable, and confident. Here was another doctor that I liked right away. We chitchatted a bit, and I found out that he liked to play tennis. When he had to step out momentarily, his assistant, Leslie, said that he was fanatical about tennis and quite good.

When he returned, I remarked that Leslie had said that he was a good tennis player for a beginner. He immediately shot darts at his assistant, and she couldn't hold back, and we all laughed hysterically. I could tell he really got a kick out this, and it really broke the ice. I find that you can very quickly tell what kind of person you are dealing with by how that person responds to a joke. Do they take themselves too seriously, or do they have a good sense of humor and a strong inner compass. I have found this to be quite effective. Of course, occasionally my strategy backfires.

Dr. Fine had already seen my MRI as a result of a connection with the MGH. As it turned out, he used to work with the head of radiation oncology at the MGH, Dr. Jay Loeffler. Dr. Fine also recommended doing radiation treatment first and then chemotherapy.

So far, we were two for two to change treatment protocol. He said that he would call the MGH neuro-oncologist after their weekly consult the next day and they would go over my case. I had never heard the term "weekly consult" before.

Apparently, every week, oncologists from many nearby hospitals get together to go over selected special cases. My situation qualified since I am an adult with a child's tumor that doesn't respond to contrast dye. My medical uniqueness was turning out to be a benefit in terms of receiving quick interest by some of the best oncologists in the Eastern United States, who are always on the lookout for something new and unusual.

This is fortunate for me, even though I wish I could have been "new and different" in some other manner, but for now, I am grateful and hopeful this will help lead to a better chance for a positive outcome.

The next stop was the National Children's Medical Center in Washington, DC, to see an oncologist specializing in pathology for children with brain cancer. We had arranged a meeting with him mainly as a result of determination, resourcefulness, and begging on Candy's part. She would frequently ask doctors, nurses, physician assistants, and interns who they would see if it were them. At one point, Candy was in one of her "Please help us" modes, and she was told by an assistant at a different hospital that the absolute best pathologist was this doctor at National Children's Medical Center. The assistant then begged Candy not to tell anyone she had said this. My guess was that she might have been speaking without authority and was taking a risk in doing so.

It turned out that the doctor we were about to see was the one everyone else deferred to regarding this particular type of cancer. We had also been told that his manner was not the most congenial and to be prepared for that.

When we entered the waiting room, I immediately felt out of place. The room was full of young children with a parent at their side. Again, one of those "What are you doing here?" moments as I delicately perched myself on one of the Lilliputian benches. When we were ushered into his office and told to wait and the doctor would be in momentarily.

We saw the walls covered with pictures of young children and many thank-you notes written in children's handwriting. Dr. Roger Paccar entered, and we introduced ourselves. I braced myself for a cold reception when I heard the first words out of Candy's mouth, "You love children, don't you?" I noticed a hint of a smile on his face and an immediate change in his demeanor. He then discussed my situation in a sensitive, caring manner.

We talked about a lot of topics in addition to my particular medical issues. In the end, he also recommended initiating my treatment with radiation therapy and not chemotherapy. He also thought we should take another look at having a resection of the malignant tumor.

He said that my survival rate would be much higher. His caveat was that the only person who could possibly attempt this was a surgeon at Brigham and Women's Hospital named Dr. Peter Black.

However, he added that his status as one of the most renowned brain surgeons in the country meant that we would probably have to wait several months before we could get an appointment with him. Candy spoke up and said that we actually had an appointment with him the next day. Dr. Paccar was astonished. He then gave us his personal pager number and said he would be at a fund-raiser tomorrow evening but to have Dr. Black page him after he sees us. All this from a doctor who had a reputation of being gruff.

> You might be wondering how we got this appointment. I have gotten to know quite a few people over the years, especially through playing golf. Sometimes it is a friend of a friend, and the relationship is once removed, but as I said before, you get to know something about a person when you are with him over a four-hour period in a competitive environment. I also tried to play hard and well and really want to win, but in golf, it is not always possible. When I hit one into the woods or sink a forty-foot putt, my reaction is pretty much the same: "Wow." Hey, it is amateur golf, and these things happen! So to get to the point, months later, my good friend told his friend (my arm's-length friend) that I have this problem. As it turned out, he had a benign tumor removed from the surgeon mentioned above and volunteered to help me get an appointment. You just never know. I am just glad I am not the type to rant and rave and throw my clubs on the golf course.

Just to get a feel for the number of balls Candy was juggling in the air at the same time, I thought I would include her March 2001 calendar.

Nicc'e Ullrich

MARCH   ≠ bring Blue Cross Card   IV [DROPERIDOL] An nausea

SUNDAY	MONDAY	TUESDAY	WEDNESDAY
	Dr. ___ Packer III Michigan Ave NW Childrens Nat. Medical Center Washington D.C. 1-202-884-2666 Audrey CNMc.org	Feb 2?	For Review ① pre / post MRI ② SDuse ③ PAIN ___ ④ What their ___ treatment plan is better than 2017 RAN
4	**5**	**6**	**7**
	NO SCHOOL **11**	NO SCHOOL **12**	NO SCHOOL **13**
		13 LAST CUMADIN TAKEN	11³⁰ SIMULATION MASS E/E + EAR register in lobby + go 2nd floor 1³⁰ ＋ Stop Cumadin Dr. LOEFFLER Cox basement Joan Coen M.D. 2nd ___ 8³⁰ RADIATION Ⓡ ride 9-1 SKID general ___
MRI 10 — Farabers Bldg RM 138 617-724-585_ __id no eating after midnight ICU **18**	__ 11³⁰ ___ 3 AM ___ ICU **19**	Hanky ride 10 ___ __ Rd. no singing LAX d ___ 5 **20**	**20** Sharma Wanda ___ PT Mya __ Dr. ___ **28**
ICU **25** Nasty Home Kelly NW Ⓡ	School sub **26** ICU TO PHILIPS	**27** Ⓡ Varndis ___ 11-12	Ⓡ Candy
NOTES Leslies line 410-955-7347 Le__ ___ 410-283-4988 Peggy @ Batander 617-724-8770	Dr. Von Coss ___ ___ @ 410-614-5055 new papers # 410-955-8764 ＊Leslie (Neuro) Dr. Burg ___ ___		

M6H ... FAX 978 526-1804 * 029387660 *

362·13·22   Email R Stecker @ Boston RM.com **MARCH**

THURSDAY	FRIDAY *VP d/c	SATURDAY
1	2	3
		RAY Home!
SPINE MRI	BONE SCAN	
9:00 CLINIC A 8	9	RAY CUT 10 HAIR
Pediatric Oncology Clinic Howard Finc 3oL-4☐-6383 Nat Institute of Health Bethesda	Dr. Cohen Brenda B+ W 16 9:45 Check blood	97668QTV# 17 Levels at Beverly
John Hopkins Bethesda Dr Parra Packer Children Lw Adm # 202-8C- AX 9746314900 RAY emergency room 22	70 NEW YORK Went Diccup 23 BLAKE 1252 Nurse Mary	FRINIGHTS 5-6 SKIING 11:00 (R) 24 1633 Broadway Corner 51st Venting MRI Nurse Nancy
Peter Pick up 9½ admitted 2232 12:00 omni start decadron (R) 29	RAY (R) 30	Kelly Packs 6:5 - 11:00 31
	Buin + 10 mcg Dr. PETER BLACK 617-732-6810	Boston 45 Francis St. 617-732-5500 3rd Floor -

MARCH 15? LV. Boston → Baltimore
Johns Hopkins + arrive 1½
8th Floor CM + Sin Center AID - 955 - 8751
drive D.C. Children (the)

MARCH 2000						
S	M	T	W	T	F	S
			1	2	3	4
5	6	7	8	9	10	11
12	13	14	15	16	17	18
19	20	21	22	23	24	25
26	27	28	29	30	31	

MARCH 2001						
S	M	T	W	T	F	S
				1	2	3
4	5	6	7	8	9	10
11	12	13	14	15	16	17
18	19	20	21	22	23	24
25	26	27	28	29	30	31

MARCH 2002						
S	M	T	W	T	F	S
					1	2
3	4	5	6	7	8	9
10	11	12	13	14	15	16
17	18	19	20	21	22	23
24	25	26	27	28	29	30
31						

MARCH 2003						
S	M	T	W	T	F	S
						1
2	3	4	5	6	7	8
9	10	11	12	13	14	15
16	17	18	19	20	21	22
23	24	25	26	27	28	29
30	31					

MARCH 2004						
S	M	T	W	T	F	S
	1	2	3	4	5	6
7	8	9	10	11	12	13
14	15	16	17	18	19	20
21	22	23	24	25	26	27
28	29	30	31			

MARCH 2005						
S	M	T	W	T	F	S
		1	2	3	4	5
6	7	8	9	10	11	12
13	14	15	16	17	18	19
20	21	22	23	24	25	26
27	28	29	30	31		

MARCH 2006						
S	M	T	W	T	F	S
			1	2	3	4
5	6	7	8	9	10	11
12	13	14	15	16	17	18
19	20	21	22	23	24	25
26	27	28	29	30	31	

Chapter 10

Strategy Adjustment

Candy and I flew back to Boston that night and then drove to Brigham and Women's Hospital the next morning to make our 9:45 a.m. appointment. Once there, we had a short wait and were then ushered into a small conference room.

Within minutes, the doctor entered. After brief introductions, he grabbed a chair and pulled it up right in front of me so that we were face-to-face, eyeball-to-eyeball. He said he had seen my most recent MRI and that there were risks to a resection, but he thought he would be able to get about 80 percent of the tumor out. He also urged us to remember that, as a brain surgeon, he might be more likely to recommend surgery.

I really appreciated his honesty. I recalled the earlier advice given by my first surgeon to be wary of having a resection attempt and the potential negative ramifications. Visions of me in a wheelchair flashed through my mind.

He stepped out briefly, and when he returned, he said that their weekly consult would be held in one hour and he would like to discuss my case with the other oncologists on the call. He suggested we come back after lunch.

Candy and I had something to eat within the hospital and returned in two hours. When we met after lunch, he told us he had just spoken to every doctor we had seen the day before and that they all said I should have radiation first and then chemotherapy. He emphasized that these doctors were the best in their field and, therefore, recommended that we follow their advice.

He further explained that going full guns with radiation would likely to be more effective than doing chemo first. Plus if I did chemo first, I might not be able to physically handle the amount of radiation that would be necessary. As strange as it may sound, I felt empowered and proud of what we had done. Candy, in particular, had started the ball rolling on this whole trip. Her persistent research had found significant evidence supporting the strategy that radiation prior to chemo was more effective. Her organization and resourcefulness in getting all these appointments was a Herculean task that I never could have done. As a result, I had confidence that we were heading down the right path. We hadn't just accepted the first treatment option presented to us.

Chapter 11

Game On # 1

When we had completed our four second opinions, we called our oncologist at MGH and notified him that we had been advised to start with radiation treatment. After one more MRI, I was set to start radiation in four days.

Then there were the logistics. My understanding was that this procedure would be an outpatient treatment five days a week for six weeks. During this time, I would be living at home. My question of whether I could drive myself from treatment and back each day was met with quizzical looks. It turned out that someone would have to drive me. This was probably a good idea, plus I would get to spend more time with Candy since she would be my designated driver. Additionally, the MGH has a special valet parking service, along with a separate entrance to the hospital for patients undergoing cancer treatment. This is located at a separate entrance in the back side of the hospital. This turned out to be very helpful, plus it was free—oh, the benefits of having cancer!

Candy and I got to my first radiation session in plenty of time for my first appointment. The location was in the same area where I had my simulation.

Once again, I was experiencing this strange feeling of being among people in various stages of physical disrepair, yet I looked perfectly normal and healthy. I had my khakis and blue blazer on. But all around me were people in hospital johnnies, some with no hair on their heads, some with scarves around their heads to hide what I guessed was their baldness. There were actually a couple of people who looked OK. I couldn't tell if they were patients awaiting treatment or relatives of those who were. Outside the main waiting area, there was a very frail-looking man lying prone on a hospital gurney oblivious to his surroundings. I feared that he did not have much of a future and felt sorry for him.

A couple of attendants were walking around with carts, offering people ginger ale, apple juice, saltines, and other bland crackers. I didn't quite understand this but caught on after a few visits. As I was brought into the treatment room, I was told that in subsequent sessions, I could bring a tape or CD to play during my radiation. The technicians set me on the bed facedown and went through a number of adjustments so that I was positioned just right. The actual treatment was over in about four minutes—no pain, no chicken wire face mask. I didn't feel a thing. I thought to myself this was going to be easy. It wouldn't be long before I found out that I was totally wrong.

On the way back home, Candy and I stopped off at a little historic spot to have a light lunch. I had a bit of a headache. When we arrived home, Candy called the oncologist to see if I could take something for it, and he recommended Tylenol.

Since I had atrial fibrillation (irregular heartbeat), I am only allowed to take acetaminophen (the ingredient used in Tylenol) since ibuprofen and other over-the-counter pain relievers thin the blood, and I am already on Coumadin (a prescription blood thinner). We proceeded through the remainder of the day uneventfully.

That came to an end quite suddenly at about midnight when I started throwing up violently over the side of the bed. In an effort to get to the bathroom, I realized I could not walk and was reduced to crawling. Candy wanted to call an ambulance to take me to the MGH, but we rethought that strategy. I felt it would take any ambulance longer to get there and that we could get to Boston more quickly if we didn't have to wait for them to arrive.

The next issue was how I was going to get down the stairs. Well, with Candy at 115 pounds and me at 205, it was obvious she couldn't carry me. Then it dawned on me to go down the stairs the same way very young children do: sitting on your rear end with legs ahead while you arms are steadying yourself. OK, good routine, and I used that method transporting myself down from the second floor and out the front stairs of the house. To add excitement, it was pouring rain outside, and the car was about twenty yards away in our gravel driveway. So I transitioned from the child's-rear-end-down-the-stairs method to hands-and-knees crawling over gravel while Candy held an umbrella over me. I was able to pull myself up into the car (very glad we didn't have a big SUV), and off we went to the MGH.

Since most people have the sense not to drive down Route 1 at 12:45 a.m. in a torrential rainstorm, there was not much traffic, and the trip only took about thirty-five minutes.

After we pulled up to the emergency entrance, Candy got out of the car to find someone to help. An attendant came out with a wheelchair and pushed me up the ramp and into the emergency room, and they both helped me off the wheelchair and onto a hospital bed.

Then two aides appeared. They helped me off the bed and supported me under each arm to see if I had the capability to walk on my own. It was quickly apparent that walking was no longer part of my repertoire. I was hooked up to an IV delivering some kind of liquid into me, but I was not sure what. Candy was there next to me the entire time and provided the attendants with information about what had just happened, the name of my neuro-oncologist, and the radiation treatment I had received earlier that day. A while later, I was given additional medication, which might have been stronger pain medication for my headache and/or potentially the drug Decadron, which is used to reduce swelling of the brain for patients who receive radiation.

By about 3:00 a.m., I was completely wiped out yet unable to sleep or get a quiet rest. I realized that six weeks more of this was going to be very tough.

I noticed that Candy had fallen asleep in the chair next to my bed. However, I had no such luck. Once again, it felt as if no one on the emergency staff even knew I existed. They were all chattering, and the radio was tuned in to some new wave music station.

I had fallen into a woozy state somewhere between conscious and semiconscious. Maybe this was all a dream. Was I really lying here in all this misery with no idea what was happening to me and no doctor in sight to ask? Whatever it was, I had reached my limit and couldn't take it anymore. I yelled out, "WILL YOU PLEASE SHUT UP!" Candy almost fell out of her chair. She went from thinking that I was out cold to hearing me yell out this primal scream and couldn't figure out what just happened. Later on, we laughed about it, but at that moment, it didn't seem so funny. To make matters worse, my interjection had absolutely no effect on the noise level.

Finally, one of the neuro-oncologists stopped by. Apparently, my horrible night was the result of my brain swelling and pressing against my skull after my first radiation treatment. Unknown to me until now is that I have a *team* of cancer specialists working on my behalf. The team includes my brain surgeon, three neuro-oncologists, three radiation oncologists, and their ancillary staff of technicians.

The technicians are very important since they implement the delivery of the radiation and have to be sure I am positioned correctly for each session. This enables the linear accelerator to bombard my brain and spine in the correct locations. As it turns out, I will be receiving full cranial and full spinal radiation five days a week for the next six weeks and the multiple proton boosts directly targeted at the tumor itself, which in radiation oncology parlance is called stereotactic radiation.

In the emergency room, the radiation oncologist, Candy, and I had a nice chat. Apparently, the swelling in my brain was so severe that I needed to go to the operating room to have a hole drilled in my skull to help relieve the pressure. A mini hose would be inserted into my skull right next to my brain to enable the liquid to flow out. What kind of liquid this was, I did not care to know, nor did I care to see. I never did, thank God. The doctor did say that the operation would be so simple that I did not need general anesthesia. In fact, I would be awake during the entire procedure, so they could ask me questions along the way: Did I feel any pain? Could I move my toes? Could I move my fingers, etc.? I had some questions of my own: What if they asked me if I could talk and I couldn't? And why would I want to be awake while someone drilled a hole in my head?

Candy was there to kiss me good-bye, so I did not have a panic attack like I did the first time around, but I was a little nervous about being conscious during the operation. I was told this would take from one to one and a half hours versus the seven-hour marathon of the first operation.

I was transported by my friends, the materials management people, to a part of the hospital I had never seen before where they left me in a hallway waiting for the doctors with the Black and Decker tools. During these "wait in the hall on the hospital gurney" sessions, I was often tempted to pipe in with my own opinion or comment on conversations going on around me, but I did not. I might startle someone or get rude glances to mind my own business. I realized that any such attempt was unlikely to be the highlight of anyone's day, so I was consistently demure. It took a lot of effort though.

After I was moved into the operating room, a nurse changed the drip bag and began to give me some sort of anesthesia, but I was still wide awake. They did some testing and asked some questions to determine if I felt any pain (which I did not), but it wasn't totally reassuring.

Once things got started, I could hear the whizzing of the drill and smelled something strange, but felt no pain. The one reassuring thing was that they were talking to me the entire time, and I could talk back. It dawned on me that the strange smell must have been from the soft tissue outside my brain. Then I had a strange sensation of something very familiar: it was like stepping on a piece of half-broken glass and hearing it crunching under your shoe. But this time it wasn't glass on the ground; it was pieces of my skull crunching as the drill bit cut through my head. I was fighting the urge to yell out to them, "Stop! Stop!" But there was no pain. When it was over, I was moved to intensive care, conscious and glad to see Candy.

I had an IV going into my arm, a tube coming out of my head to collect the stuff draining out of my brain, and a monitor connected to my heart to monitor my heartbeat. The whole thing was a pretty pathetic sight.

The next morning, a Saturday, I received my next treatment. A Saturday? Yes. When we arrived downstairs, there was no one there other than a few workers on ladders removing ceiling tiles and threading multiple large spools of wires all over the place. I hoped that this electrical work was not going to affect my radiation treatment, and I also thought there must be a pretty large concern about getting me back on track, which was OK with me and signified they weren't fooling around or taking things lightly. Afterward, I was returned to my room to get some rest. So I got some quiet time, and other than the usual take my blood, give a urine sample, etc., it was pretty boring stuff. I spoke with Candy, and she was doing things with the kids, and everything seemed to be going well there. The next morning, I was wheeled down to the same radiation treatment area, but this was a whole new experience. I was accompanied by two nurses at all times, and Candy was allowed to accompany them. Apparently, I did not have a great night and looked like I was at death's door. I arrived on the transportable bed with tubes coming out of my head, tubes coming out of my arms, an IV drip bag hanging from above, and a "crash kit" on my lap.

I sensed that the doctors in charge of my treatment were worried about me having a heart attack, that A-Fib thing again, and didn't want to take any chances. Since this was not a pleasant sight for everyone else waiting for treatment, I was pushed over to an area behind a curtain and out of sight until it was my turn. Earlier, I discussed my first treatment and the old geezer who looked like he was one foot away from the grave. Well, I wished I looked as good as him!

I was laughing to myself about how quickly things changed. Everyone always gets a kick out of it, and it just really cracks me up—what the heck are you going to do? Laugh was the only thing I could think of, even now.

For some reason, I was returned to a different room, just the next one down, still without a roommate, so it was fine with me.

Apparently, my mother-in-law, who was a fabulous woman, had the telephone number to my room. We had always gotten along terrifically, and she used to joke about pulling out my hair if I wasn't treating her daughter properly. It was just an ongoing thing we had. She hadn't been informed of my room change and called my previous room number. A man answered, and the first words out of her mouth were "If you do not get out of that bed, I am going to come over and pull the rest of your hair out." Candy's mother told her this, and they both laughed for about a week.

I was put on pretty close watch, and a physical therapist was called in to try to get me back into walking mode. Eventually, I was assisted by a therapist with a walker (you know, one of those devices old people use) as an aid to help me as I spent time rehabbing and simulating walking down the corridor. I continued to make progress in between radiation treatments. I wasn't allowed to leave my room without first being set up with the walker and rolling IV stand. Following my theory that "rules are guidelines," I began picking up the walker as I shuffled past the nurses' stand. Of course, I was showing off for Candy, but I didn't want to be using that thing longer than necessary. On a subsequent call with my mother-in-law, she asked how I was doing. I replied, "Well, except that I never thought I would be using a walker before you." She got a kick out of that.

On a sad note, she passed away in December 2010. She was ninety-six years old. She was a wonderful woman of charm, grace, and a gift to be able to warm the hearts of others. She is deeply missed by all.

As my ambulatory capabilities improved, I was allowed to go home with Candy after each treatment. We got into the groove of driving in every day and got the special valet parking handled by the parking attendant Mack who over time became a good friend.

As a sidebar, I recently saw him (fall of 2010) when I was in for one of my checkups. He is one of those ageless people and is always happy. We recognized each other right away. He hadn't aged at all, and I am sure I looked about twenty years older. We gave each other a big hug and talked about family for a while—he has six children! I admire him. He is making life easier for people who need it, and he is a pro at what he does.

Candy and I continued with the routine. I usually did the drive on these initial trips because it was one of the few things I could control at this point. The reasoning was simple: when I was sitting down, I didn't have any walking issues, plus this was a fairly new car, and I hadn't quite had the courage to "release the keys" to Candy yet. However, in mid-April, with fatigue and weakness rapidly increasing due to effects of the radiation, I handed the keys over to Candy. During the next trip down for treatment, as we approached a stoplight very close to the MGH—*boom!*

We were rear-ended by a cement truck at a stoplight, and it started pushing us forward. I yelled over to Candy, "Jam on the brakes! Jam on the brakes!"

She yelled back, "I am, I am!" while she had both feet full force on the brake so much so that she was just about prone on her back. All that happened was the cement truck kept on pushing us (tires screeching and smoking) for about half a block and then it stopped. We were bracing for an argument from the cement truck driver, but as it turned out, he was very apologetic. He said he was having problems with his brakes and was having a bad day. Candy and I looked at each other. *If he only knew.*

Candy pulled the car to the side of the road, and some construction guys working nearby helped pick up various pieces of the rear end of the car and put them in the trunk. I did not want to miss my radiation treatment, so I said good-bye and gingerly shuffled across the street the remaining one hundred yards or so to the hospital. From a distance, I could see the flashing blue lights coming to Candy's rescue.

This seemed to be the point at which each subsequent radiation session sapped my strength and energy more and more. My first radiation treatment was on March 21 and it was now the third week of April, and I was approaching the toughest part: the regular radiation plus the proton boost that would directly target the tumor itself.

After one of these sessions, Candy and I were approaching an elevator and noticed a sign nearby that read "If you are having difficulty handling fatigue as a result of cancer treatment, please come to group session to get help at room B on the sixth floor at 4:00 p.m." We looked at each other and said we were too tired to go!

My last radiation treatment was on April 30 followed by another MRI and a meeting with the neuro-oncologist to assess my status.

During most all of my meetings with my neuro-oncologist, we went through a similar procedure, which included various tests to provide immediate feedback. I consistently flunked all of them. When needles were poked into my ankles, I felt nothing. When a metal two-pronged vibration tool was banged on a table and held against my ankle, I felt nothing. When a rubber triangle attached to a metal handle was tapped just below my kneecap, I had no reflex reaction. Sometimes I asked him to repeat the process because I just could not believe I couldn't feel any of these things. The most important and always my weakest event was the heel-to-toe walk. You know, like the sobriety test given to people suspected of driving under the influence. Almost ten years later, I still dread the thought of getting pulled over for a bad taillight or some other minor infraction and being asked to take that test. I know that even dead sober, there is still no way I could pass that test even now!

During these past six weeks of outpatient MRIs, CAT scans, and blood work, I would arrive at home wiped out. I didn't have enough energy to read, talk to anyone, or watch TV. I just wanted to lie down and not move. Plus it was much safer than walking around. We even named a couch in the library the Cancer Couch, where I spent a lot of my time. There were two episodes when I passed out: One while I was walking across the kitchen and bumped into the ironing board, taking everything down with me as I fell. The iron just missed hitting my head. The second time, I was reaching for the door handle to let our dog in when suddenly I found myself looking up from the floor wondering how I got there. I had never experienced anything like this before, and it was scary. It made me feel helpless, frail, and weak. Fortunately, it did not happen again.

In both instances, my younger daughter, Hadley, had been home along with my wife, and she was the one who had to help me get up. Just halfway through the fourth grade, she never cried or panicked or showed any fear. She knew I needed some help and did what she had to with a reassuring calmness.

Hadley was the one who was home that entire year and experienced hands on what I was going through all the way to the end of treatment when I was at my weakest. I never asked her how it felt to see me so weak having grown up with me being so strong physically and emotionally and always there for my family. During this time, the roles were definitely reversed. She had an English assignment at that time to write about someone who was important to her. She chose me. Her short essay below was sent to us by her teacher and brings tears to my eyes every time I read it. I had been trying to handle my own crisis with dignity and courage in hopes that my children would see this and be more equipped to handle their own setbacks as they progressed through life. This essay became one of the most inspiring things I have ever read. My young ten-year-old showed a level of trust, belief, and courage that was hard to comprehend. It astounds me every time I read it. I wonder who was really teaching whom how to handle adversity.

My dad, Ray is very important to me. He has made me laugh when I feel sad. He once made me cry because I was so happy by him getting better, and walking around the room with a fabulous smile on his face.

He has raised me since I was born. My dad also helps my whole family be happy.

Ray loves teaching me anything I am curious about, such as golf, swimming, or giving me horse-back riding tips.

My dad helps me believe that I can do almost anything, and that it might just take time. I know that he can do anything from horse-back riding, to fighting cancer. My great dad showed me that it is possible.

I love playing with him. We laugh, and have a promising time. The two of us play mini-soccer and we pass around the ball in lacrosse, and field hockey. My dad and I love to hang around with each other, even if we are just watching T.V.

I know that I can tell my dad anything, and he will try to understand, and relate to the problem or concern.

I love my dad so, so much. He is one of the many important people to me, and he always will be.

I had started radiation therapy six weeks earlier at a svelte and athletic six feet two inches and 205 pounds and was now a pathetic and weakened 160 pounds without one piece of hair on my entire body. So much for getting on the cover of *Men's Fitness* magazine! A good friend of ours told Candy that she needed to get me some "cancer clothes" since the clothing I had was so loose they made me look like I was sick. That was an understatement if I ever heard one. Anyway, she did, and it was an improvement.

As for work during this period, I was, and am, fortunate that I have my own business with several very talented people. I tried to make it into the office as much as I could. The fact that it was nearby certainly helped. There were days that I would go in, stay for two or three hours, and come home. Some days I felt strong enough to stay longer. Some days I would go in, sit at my desk, put my head down, take a few breaths and pack up, and come home to the Cancer Couch.

Everyone in the company stepped up to the plate and kept things going. This just speaks to the quality of the people I work with. At the end of the day, it is always about the people. Where they went to school, what grades they got, or how many initials follow their name doesn't matter—it's their genuineness and what's in their hearts that count!

I feel this is true with both professional colleagues and personal friends.

At this point, I was in a very weakened state. I had approximately two weeks during which I had time for another MRI, doctor's visits, and some quality time with the Cancer Couch. Then I would be all set to start chemotherapy treatment. I couldn't wait—yikes!

The other side of me viewed this as a milestone—I was at the halfway point and headed for the homestretch. I was thinking, *Don't back off now, keep it at full throttle*. Unfortunately, "full throttle" for me wasn't what it used to be. My bravado was definitely fading. I was weak and exhausted and, "How in the world am I going to do this?" began to creep into my mind. This was a thought I did not share with Candy.

Chapter 12

Game On # 2

Chemotherapy

It occurred to me that the use of the word "therapy" tacked on to the end of words like "chemo" or "radiation" is a bit of an insult or even rubbing salt in the wound. Massage therapy makes sense: you end up feeling relaxed, soothed, and stress-free. There is no possible way you can attach those results to radiation therapy and chemotherapy. Tense, debilitated, and a nervous wreck maybe, but not relaxed, soothed, and stress-free, that's for sure. Nonetheless, I am about to become very familiar with the words cisplatin, etoposide, vincristine, and cyclophosphamide, also known as Cytoxan. Why someone decided to use 62 percent of the entire alphabet for the name of one drug is beyond me, especially when they have a second shorter name already set up. Perhaps this was decided after the fact since many people like myself or even oncologists themselves were challenged to pronounce the word.

I apologize for getting technical on you, but when you are in the process of going through a meat grinder, you at least want to know what kind of chemical characters you are getting mixed up with. The important thing to remember is that vincristine is the nasty one.

There were three (eight-week) cycles with duration variances, depending on my ability to recover from each chemo treatment—as you can see, the concept of therapy doesn't quite jibe with my mind-set. For the first week, I was in the hospital for five days and received chemo for *nineteen hours a day for five days straight*. Of course, at that time, for all I knew, I could have been getting off easily. It could have been worse, I could have been given chemo twenty-four hours a day, but why hold back? What's five more hours when you have already had nineteen?

Afterward, I would get some time off to recover after which I would have chemo twice a week (two days in a row on an outpatient basis for four hours each day). I was thinking that if I was going through this cycle three times and the cancer didn't get killed, I probably would.

How was I able to get all this chemo and more without destroying the veins in my arms where one would expect the infusion (I am getting a knack for the lingo now) to enter? Answer: a portable catheter, or port for short. This is a quasi-flat squeezable device that necessitates one of those "mini" procedures during which the apparatus was implanted under *my* skin near the chest area. Normally, much of my very manly chest hair would have to be shaved off, but since I did not have any chest hair anymore, or any hair at all for that matter, this was not necessary and facilitated things for the white-gown-attired professionals—I am so glad I could help. Of course, I was wide awake as SpongeBob SquarePants was inserted into my chest through a newly established gash on my pristine, hairless body. It was a very interesting procedure to watch, and there was no glass-crunching special effects to shake up my already fragile equilibrium. However, they did leave SpongeBob's wiggly hands hanging out of my chest in a good position to dock with the chemo transfer tubing I would be utilizing over the next few months.

Chemo was administered to me in my new room, which was in a different location in the hospital. Unfortunately, the accommodations for this part of my treatment were a few notches below the former space I had when I first came to the hospital. As I entered my new home for the week, I noticed two beds with a curtain between them, so it looked like I was going to have a roommate. I decided to take the bed nearest the door so that I could escape in a hurry if necessary. It was just like summer camp: the first person to arrive gets their choice, unless the second person arrives and is bigger and meaner than you. Well, within a few minutes, my roommate arrived. I looked at him as he walked by. He was not bigger and meaner; he looked skinnier, scarier, and meaner. I immediately felt shaky, and then I recognized him. He was the guy with tattoos, maybe two or three teeth missing, and crazy eyes—just like the guy in the movie *Deliverance,* and I do not mean Burt Reynolds.

What was I going to do? I could not imagine going to sleep with this guy on the other side of the curtain. He walked over to the other side of the room, sat down, turned his head, then stared at me for almost thirty seconds without one blink of his eyes. I had to get out of there. I had enough things to worry about. He was probably a very nice guy and was going through some horrible situation just like me, but I could not stay there. It was just one of those "trust your instincts" kinds of situations. I went to the nurses' station (I was somewhat mobile at this point) and explained my situation and how I felt. The nurse asked me what room number I was in. She looked at a chart, then at me, and set me up in another room. I felt a little bit like a wimp, but you know what, at that stage, that is exactly what I was, and I did not care. I just wanted to feel safe. Then I thought maybe she knew something because there was not any hesitation on her part to move me to a different room. For the next five days, I went through the drill. The nineteen hours of chemo was split up as follows: sixteen hours on one drug and then a transition to the second drug for the next three hours. This transfer was as quick as a relay racer handing off the baton to the next runner. It was very interesting that with every infusion, the nurses were always wearing extra thick rubber gloves to protect themselves from the toxic chemicals that they were force-feeding into my body. This did mess with my mind a little bit, but it was what it was. So there was a lot of monotony, boredom, and loneliness over the next five days. I was too tired to read and too tired to watch much TV, and really, how much of *The Jerry Springer Show* or *Judge Judy* can anyone watch?

Candy came to visit almost every day, which was great, and I had other visitors from time to time. I occasionally tried to get some sleep, but with tubes coming out of my chest and arms, it was complicated. It was not as if I could just roll over or switch from one side to the other. With my luck, I would end up ripping everything apart, which I am sure would be a big mess and they would have to call the hazardous waste squad! Other than that, I kept track of every nurse that came in, every time they drew my blood (through a vein in my arm, not the port), and the drip rate of the different chemo drugs. The two drugs I got during this first cycle of treatment were etoposide and vincristine.

I was given vincristine, the real nasty one, for sixteen hours. I ended up getting 309 hours of chemo pumped into my veins over the next few months; 240 of it or 78 percent of which was the mean stuff. The effects of which (as I later realize) will remain with me for the rest of my life. It's the gift that keeps on giving. I was allowed to go home but not just to lie in bed, though I did get to spend some quality time on my favorite piece of furniture again—the Cancer Couch. It turned out I needed treatment to help with my treatment. Similar to a spy movie where the captured villain is tortured in an effort to extract information, only he is so beaten up he might not make it. He is then revived to the degree that he has recovered enough so that they can start torturing him again. You wouldn't want to kick a guy when he is down. Wait until he is on one knee, *then* kick him. Just as I was at one of my low points, I received something in the mail that motivated me. It was a personal note from Lance Armstrong! My younger daughter's teacher had a friend who was on the USPS cycling team with Lance Armstrong, who then wrote me this note.

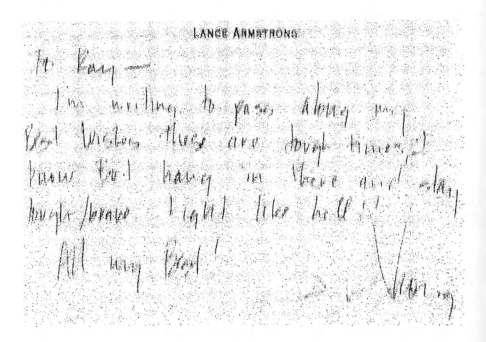

I do, of course, want to make it through all the treatments, so anything that helps me to handle the next session is fine with me. Additionally, I sense that if I am ever at the point where the doctors think I cannot physically withstand the treatment, they will dial it down. I do not want this to happen as it might lower my chances for survival.

At home, the recovery procedure is as follows: Neupogen shots every day, alternating left arm and right arm on the upper outside of my biceps, just below my shoulder. The administrator of this was my wife, Candy. The hospital showed her how to do it, and fortunately, she was a quick learner. The shots hurt; I was obviously still in wimp mode. She would grab the outer part of my bicep and pinch it to create a good spot to jab me with the needle. At first I thought that she might be enjoying this—her chance to let me have it—but I could tell that she felt sad during this process and had questioned her role. Outwardly she handled it like a pro.

Candy was busy ferrying the girls around to various places and events, which occasionally necessitated a stand-in to deliver the injections. A good friend of ours who had been a nurse earlier in her life volunteered. Our family room has windows facing the front stairs approaching the house, and just before Susan inserted the needle, I saw a woman approaching the front door who glanced over at us as she made her way up the stairs to the door. This would not normally be a noteworthy occurrence except for the fact that I did not have a shirt on! I had taken it off because I couldn't get it rolled up high enough to expose the location for the needle entry. So I opened the door *topless* and said, "Oh hi, to a woman who was delivering slip covers." Apparently she knew Candy was away visiting her mother and wondered what her husband was doing home in the middle of the day with his shirt off with a woman who was not his wife sitting on a couch. There was a "Fine, good to see you," and off she went.

I still wonder about the phone calls that must have gone around town. Candy asked why I had taken my shirt off, and I told her. Her "Yeah, right" response hinted at some disbelief, but when I saw her smile, I knew she was kidding.

During this break in the action, I also had stem cell harvesting, the obligatory MRI, and a complete blood transfusion. Separately during this process, I also had seventeen vials of blood removed and not through the port (danger of chemo contamination). I have had as many as five or six drawn before, but seeing that many stacked up together was a startling sight. This procedure didn't exactly ramp up my energy level either, but it was supposed to help me get through the upcoming treatments, and it probably did.

From a food standpoint, I began to have cravings: Italian subs for three or four days, then cheese steak subs, and then not much of an appetite or an extreme aversion to some foods.

The next four months, it was pretty much the same routine: the big week with ninety-five hours of chemo, then two to three weeks of recovery; then two outpatient days, four hours of chemo a day, recovery for two to three weeks; and start all over again. In addition to the Neupogen shots, Procrit shots were added to the mix (for anemia), which was a new item to deal with. I was also prescribed other medication to increase salt retention and another one to prevent potential infections.

During this time, when I wasn't in the hospital, I tried to participate in as many normal activities as I could—birthdays, children's sporting events, family dinners. At the end of each, I was always exhausted. My oldest daughter's graduation from elementary school was set for mid-June.

It was supposed to be a happy, stress-free occasion, but on this very sunny summerlike day, stress was in the air. A beautiful tent had been set up, and the graduates were seated in front and off to the right of the temporary stage. In a very kind gesture, the school had reserved seats for us, including my terrific mother-in-law (who was in her early eighties), in the front row just ahead of the first row within the tented area. As time began to pass and the direction of the sun shifted, the heat became unbearable. I looked over at my mother-in-law, who was quite petite. I thought she might keel over at any moment. I wasn't even sure I would be able to make it through the ceremony and couldn't imagine how she was going to.

I felt so sorry for Candy. I could see the look on her face—the fear that both her mother and husband would collapse at the same time and possibly never get up again. We did make it through, however. Candy helped me to a shady area, and her sister helped her mother to the shade as well. We both got some water, and everything worked out all right. It was the longest, most excruciating, and hottest graduation I had ever attended. I know it was much worse for Candy.

Once back at our house and after more water and some rest, Candy and I just looked at each other, shaking our heads. It would have been nice to have had a stress-free graduation, but it wasn't in the cards. And in the end, I was just glad to be there, and I know Candy was too.

I continued with chemo, more MRIs, frequent blood draws, cardiologist visits, and of course, visits with my neuro-oncologist. By the way, I still flunked all the tests he gave me. I think passing these is a requirement before I will be able to put my pants on standing up! Life continues to go on. My youngest daughter was entering the fifth grade, and my oldest daughter was entering her first year of high school. This for her meant Phillips Academy, a secondary school in Andover, Massachusetts. She was thrilled and excited as we drove her there.

She found her dorm, and an eager group of students quickly helped us unpack the car and carry everything to her room on the second floor. That was good for me since navigating a flight of stairs was very difficult, and carrying anything upstairs was not within my capabilities. They all seemed cheery and happy to meet Kelly. Candy and I did not want to meddle, so we said our good-byes, and Kelly went off to explore her new world.

A little later in the fall, we visited her for Parents Weekend. I would not be done with treatment until November, so I still had more treatment to go after seeing her. There was a whole schedule of events for us with and without our daughter. After we had toured some of the campus and attended a couple of abbreviated classes, we headed over to the library. In the lobby, I found a chair and sat down. I felt very weak and did not think I could continue.

Candy came over and remarked that I did not look very good. She wanted to call campus security to take me to the school infirmary. I did not want to make a big deal about this. Kelly arrived at the scheduled time to join us and offered to walk me to her dorm, and I could take a nap in her room. She got me a fresh bottle of water and physically assisted me to her room across campus. I knew I couldn't have made it without her help. It was difficult to think of myself as being so weak and feeble that I just could not walk another step.

I fell asleep for about two hours. When she and Candy returned, I felt better and able to continue for the remaining portion of the day. I was disappointed that Kelly had to do this for me. I didn't want her to have to take care of her dad the first time she would be introducing me to her friends and teachers. I didn't want to be a burden. After all, this was supposed to be a day and weekend about her, not about me. She just took it right in stride, almost as if her helping me was the most important thing she could do that weekend. I will never forget it.

After my last chemo treatment at the end of October, I continued on with Procrit shots and Neupogen shots through November.

During my chemotherapy treatment, I periodically received testing to see if my cancer showed any signs of spreading to my spine. This procedure, called a lumbar puncture, involves inserting a needle the length of a pole vault (OK, I may be exaggerating a little here, but that's what it seemed like) into a very small space between the third and fourth vertebrae of the spine. I was expecting the worst, but the first test was completed without incident. A month or so later, I was tested again—possibly by a sadist, a blind person, or a beginner. After three attempts with no success, the stabbing of the needle against pure bone or the nerves in my spinal cord was more than I could take. I tried not to complain, but when the technician (doctor) commented, "Why are you sweating so much?" I said, "Because you are not getting the needle in the right place, and I have to take a break." The pain was excruciating. Eventually, the procedure was completed by another physician.

I got an MRI just before Thanksgiving and a follow-up visit with my neuo-oncologist shortly thereafter. I almost always fell asleep in the MRI tube during the forty-five-plus-minute time I was in there. Somehow, it was relaxing for me, getting away from everything in a little cocoon all by myself. Sometimes, I imagined all the banging and clicking to be at the rhythm to a song during a dream I was having.

This became a regular routine every three months: MRI, then follow-up with my lead oncologist, Tracy Batchelor, to monitor my posttreatment condition and for any sign of reoccurrence or spreading of the cancer. He would perform the same battery of tests, which I continued until a few years later at which time I passed a couple of them. I never got a passing grade for the heel-to-toe walk and still don't, but at least I am here to talk about it. When I asked him if I would be all right after a couple of months, he bluntly told me that it would "most likely take years and with no exact determination of what recovery will be."

I had thought that all those other people must be wimps. As it turned out, I was little quick on the draw with that thought.

Chapter 13

Recovery, Short-Term

Now what? Where were all those medical professionals and the supporting cast I needed almost every day? Who was going to be monitoring me? What was I going to do without SpongeBob SquarePants and his wiggly legs dangling out of my chest? I was not feeling any better; I was exhausted and taking medications with stickers warning me not to operate heavy machinery because they could make me drowsy, as if I was not drowsy enough already! Plus, I still couldn't put my pants on while standing up. For some reason, that was important to me.

I have had a lot of myself being stripped away during the past year, and having to sit down to put my pants on was not helping my self-esteem. I was not heading in a good direction. I felt like I was getting depressed—me depressed? How could that happen to a person who has more energy and optimism than anyone? I was losing my sense of self, and it dawned on me—no wonder, it was because I was not myself, and I didn't know if I ever would be again.

I realized I needed help. I was sitting in our house in a rather downtrodden mental and physical state, and Candy said she was going to call the MGH and that I had to see someone. I quickly said that I couldn't agree more. Years ago, I would have said that only weak people saw therapists, but it was crystal clear at this point that I was certifiably in the very weak people club and could probably be its president!

Candy made the call and said, "There is an opening tomorrow or the day after. Which would you like?" My exact reply was, "How about tomorrow because I probably won't be able to find a gun by then." Apparently, my voice was loud enough so the person on the other end of the line could hear me. Her response to Candy was, "I can't wait to meet the two of you."

Apparently, the posttreatment specialist (my term) or social worker (the official term) is part of the package deal. This person is dedicated to brain cancer patients exclusively.

Since I am an analogy guy, I will put it this way. Often, when you buy or lease an automobile, the dealers throw in free maintenance for the life of the car. In this case, the powers that be throw in free mental and emotional care and maintenance for the duration of the life of you. As with automobiles, lifespan and maintenance levels vary, depending on use, damage during use, and any other unforeseen circumstances. This turned out to be a benefit I took advantage of regularly over the next ten years and continue to this day.

The PTS is a term I made up and has only significance for me. I always thought of a social worker as a specialized, accredited professional who usually helped people who had a family crisis of some sort (divorce, substance abuse, problem children, etc.).

Certainly a very valuable and much-needed service, but it never occurred to me to link social worker and cancer survivor complications together. However, as I write this, it occurs to me that having brain cancer is, in fact, a family crisis—a huge family crisis.

The first session was with Candy, me, and the social worker. Her office was in a part of the hospital away from any medical treatment areas, in the middle of a bland hallway with linoleum tiles and windowless doors. Candy's knock on the door was quickly answered by a woman about my age—maybe slightly older. I liked her right away. All she did was work with brain cancer patients, and her knowledge, empathy, and professionalism rang true. I knew I could trust her, and as a result, the tears flowed. I was flat out exhausted and deeply saddened and regretful for what I had put Candy through, and it pained me to have her see me this way—so weakened and so debilitated compared to man she knew. The impact on both of us, seeing the effects of my very soul being ripped out over so many months and then finally having the ability (behind closed doors) to grieve deeply for each other, turned Candy and me into emotional wrecks.

How could I have piled so much pain and misery onto the person I loved most in the world? Without Candy, I am only half a human being. I was supposed to protect her from that type of horror, but I did not, and I could not, and that is what made it worse.

We had protected each other's psyche for a year and never realized the pressure that had been building up until now. We had been able to help each other, but no one had been able to help us. Candy, especially, had been totally on her own, crying herself to sleep night after night and with the added responsibility of maintaining as much normalcy as she could for the children. So seated in a little room with a complete stranger, we cried our eyes out for almost an hour. It was liberating. It wasn't a complete healing, but it was a start. From that point on, we had many sessions together.

There was plenty of crying, plenty of laughing, and sometimes both. I remember well her telling me that it was OK, I did not have to be strong all the time.

A lot of stress and pressure were released during those sessions. One time, when I told her I was going to work every day, she looked at me in amazement and said that most people would either be in the hospital or in bed given the treatment I had received.

In the initial stages, Candy accompanied me quite often in these sessions, especially when I was scheduled for an MRI and review by the neuro-oncologist as my visits with her were usually scheduled immediately afterward. I always assumed there would be no indications of recurrence or abnormalities, but Candy was always on pins and needles until we got the signal that everything was OK and that the cancer was not spreading. On only one occasion did the results of an MRI indicate otherwise. There were a few blood coagulations, for lack of a better term. We were told that this was not unusual and was less than might be expected at this point in time.

As a precaution, my next scheduled MRI was moved up by a number of months. Again, I liked the way this was being handled: taking a proactive preventative approach instead of waiting for the next regularly scheduled scan.

At one point, my PTS suggested that attending a group session she was holding at a Lahey Clinic might be helpful. This is a satellite facility on the North Shore not far from my house. I readily agreed to attend, thinking that it might be helpful to talk with others in a situation similar to mine—people with brain cancer. There were about twelve to fifteen of us sitting in a circle. Everyone was in some manner of physical disrepair. One man, about my age, had obviously lost most of the use of his left leg; others were reed thin, and many of the women had scarves covering their heads. We were asked to introduce ourselves and briefly describe a little bit about our personal circumstances, treatment received, and concerns. As I heard the short version of what I knew must have been long stories, I could feel my heart sinking deeper and deeper into a mournful pit. There was a young woman who had recently been married prior to her cancer diagnosis and related how her new husband had not signed up for this and how awful she felt about it, all the while tears dripping down from her eyes.

I probably looked the least damaged of the group, and I was able to mask my balance problem by walking very slowly. The hair I had remaining on my head had returned in a patchwork pattern, but at least I had some. (I temporarily opted for the crew cut look, which happened to return to popularity just in time.) Besides, for a guy, it doesn't really matter, but it's different for a woman, and I felt sorry for them. As I went through my treatment protocol, I could see people staring at me in disbelief. I'm sure they were wondering, How could this guy have gone through all that treatment and still be able to even speak? As we all know, looks can be deceiving. Here I was the person who had received the most aggressive treatment, yet I looked in better condition than everyone else. I did not feel comfortable.

I felt guilty, and I did not return. I told my PTS that it was difficult for me to go through all that and did not think that I could handle it on a regular basis. The core issue here for me was that cancer was already a big part of my life, but I didn't want it to be the focus of my life. I wanted to minimize it as much as possible. However, much of my heart went out to these courageous people along with the respect I had for all of them. I felt that hearing about their pain was not going to help me climb out of the deep black hole I was in. Fortunately, she understood my position, acknowledging that group counseling does not work for everyone.

Things continued for a while with various annoyances. Mostly, I was trying to figure who Ray Stecker was going to be AC compared to who he was BC. I was hoping that Ray AC wouldn't be that different from Ray BC. But I was wrong.

Chapter 14

Recovery, Long-Term Now What?

Once I got beyond the short-lived quasi euphoria over being done with treatment, I slowly morphed from the immediate recovery phase (one to two years or so) to the long-term perpetual ramifications of dealing with the physical and emotional aftereffects of all the treatment I received during the last ten months in 2001. There is no set structure or path once you are out of the barn, and therefore, I did not know what to expect. There were some pluses and some minuses. On the plus side, I did not have the total debilitating weakness I experienced for the first year or so after treatment. Also, my weight came back, so I did not look so emaciated.

Whatever hair returned to my head came back in patches, and fortunately, the marine haircut had come into vogue, so I decided to keep it permanently short. I viewed this as a neutral since it really didn't matter, plus it would save me money on shampoo.

On the negative side, the most obvious was my balance. I would think about every step I took and never got up or down the stairs without holding on to a banister—even today.

For those of you who play golf, I went from a 7 handicap to a 19, not exactly something to cheer about, but I was happy simply to be able to play, and it has improved since then. But it is just golf after all and not a big deal. I continue to work on it, enjoy it, and try to be as competitive as I can.

I was with my younger daughter, who now has even more insight than when she wrote that brief essay when she was in fourth grade.

Hadley had come home to visit for the weekend. As she was packing up for the flight to return to college, I noticed she was taking quite a bit of extra stuff back to school, and I went down to the basement slowly, cautiously, and holding the banister to retrieve an extra LL Bean Duffle. The extra items she was packing were not the typical shoes, scarves, or jeans that I had become accustomed to. I had learned over the years to stay clear of any comments or opinions on the quantity or style of my daughters' wardrobe (unless complimentary) as this was my wife's domain and certainly not mine. But on this occasion, something was different. I noticed all sorts of stenciled canvas, purple sunglasses, odd-shaped cups, and other gift-type accessories.

My daughter informed me that all these items were for her "littles." Before I could ask, Hadley explained she was the big sister to two new freshmen girls who were in the process of joining her sorority and these items were welcoming gifts/favors for them. One item in particular caught my eye—a plaque with a quote perfectly etched that was meant to signify the essence of the sorority.

> "From the outside looking in, you can never understand it. From the inside looking out, you can never explain it."

It hit me instantly: This is one of the reasons why depression sets in after treatment and why ongoing/long-term recovery is so difficult. You are just so alone regardless of how many family and friends you have for support. The medical community has not yet learned how to address the increasingly longer lifespan of cancer survivors. It is a strange dynamic: you are physically present, but emotionally and cognitively, it is tough.

Everyone is glad to see you out and about, but they are not sure if they should inquire about your status or prognosis.

I am on the highway of life again but relegated to being a right-lane driver—in the slow lane, close to the breakdown lane. I can be the King of the Right Lane! I really want to be pulling into the left lane, so I can whip by these slowpokes, but I know that is where I need to be for now. And I think "now" really means forever. This is where my PTS gave me one of her gems of advice, and it comes in the form of an analogy (right up my alley).

She said,

> "Ray, here is the analogy: It's as if your whole life you had planned to move to Italy when you got older and that time finally came. For the last few years you had done a lot of research, mapped out where you are going to live, learned the language, made plans for all of the little towns and cafés to visit. Departure day arrived, you are all packed and ready to go. You are very excited for this wonderful next stage of your life, and off you go on the plane headed to Italy. However, something goes wrong with the plane, and it has to land in Holland, and you are never getting to Italy. So you have learn to appreciate what Holland has to offer."

I think about that frequently. It is not a panacea, but it helps a lot. Holland does have windmills, lots of tulips, and Amsterdam is the home of the Heineken beer brewery.

It is not Italy, but I will learn to appreciate it. After all, it could have been worse: the plane could have crashed!

Of course, it is not that easy, and why would I think it would be? Being optimistic can be a real pain in the neck sometimes. Just when you think you are getting the hang of things and proud of yourself for having made some progress, there is a fast curveball being thrown at you, but you cannot move, and then—*bam!*—it hits you right on the head!

That curveball came in March of 2008, a little over seven years since the completion of my treatment. That's when my hearing began to free-fall. I did not know if this was a just a temporary, unrelated condition or if my cancer had come back with a vengeance. I went to Massachusetts Eye and Ear Infirmary to have a hearing test followed up by an appointment with my neuro-oncologist, who confirmed the hearing loss was collateral damage as the result of radiation treatment. I asked him why I wasn't aware that this might happen.

His response was that "most people did not live long enough to have the problem"! Wow, how was I supposed to respond to that? Very simply: *Well, I guess I must be Superman!* I just couldn't believe it. Now I had to deal with this and add another doctor to my current stable of physicians I see on a regular basis. I have been seeing so many doctors for so long, some are becoming personal friends.

Fortunately, my timing has a few benefits. In addition to being in the zeitgeist with my shaved head, I am now privy to some significant technology in the form of high-tech hearing aids that are Bluetooth compatible. These new devices mean my TV at home and phones at the office function wirelessly with sound channeled directly into my ears. I could handle a regular phone to some degree, but this makes the whole process clearer and seamless. The cell phone has the same benefits if I need it. So not a big deal other than the expense—ouch!—of these high-tech gadgets and the occasional swapping out of dead hearing aid batteries, occasionally at inopportune times.

Once in a while, I mourn for the old me, but I do not brood over it. I do not allow those feelings to overwhelm me. In the scheme of things, what I experienced pales with what many people have gone through. I have never been to war and been exposed to the gruesome horrors that exist there. I have never had a child predecease me. I do not know if I could survive in those circumstances.

I think it is healthy to acknowledge who I was, who I am now, and all that my family and I went through. I am quite sure my PTS would agree with me. When you think about it, we all go through this process in one way or another. No one can do what they could when they were younger—it's called aging! In my case, this metamorphosis occurred over a few months instead of decades. I feel as if someone hit the Fast-Forward button by mistake and threw in a couple of extra zingers for good measure. I am more than ten years distanced from active treatment, but the CD part just kept hanging on and won't let go. I wanted to shove the aftereffects, the "collateral damage" of cancer, into the corner for one massive lifetime timeout. Unfortunately, in most cases, it doesn't work that way. So what are you going to do? "Improvise, adapt, and overcome." That came from a Clint Eastwood movie, but I like it, and he is right.

It is a challenge I take on every day, but everyone has challenges. In my case, I may have gotten an extra dose, but someone *up there* must have thought I could handle it. As it turned out, I could, I am able, and I will. Mother Teresa put it well when she said, "I know God won't give me anything I can't handle. I just wish He didn't trust me so much."

My heart goes out to those of you or your loved ones who have or are about to go through their battle with cancer. For some, treatment will be simple and easy with no chemotherapy or radiation; for most, it will not. My advice is to stay as positive as you can, stay optimistic, be your own advocate, and do not give up. Somehow I think your body reacts to this.

Be strong and brave. Fight like hell.

The author with his wife, ten years after treatment

Epilogue

I could not have gotten through this without Candy. The devastation I know she felt after my surgery—her whole life shattered, like a glass pitcher smashed on the floor. The countless lonely, crying nights. Her courage in keeping our children moving forward and positive through this whole ordeal. Her courage in never letting me know how much she was suffering, her perpetual smile and commitment to me. Her ability, strength, and organization in planning and executing the "Invasion of Normandy" (the visits to all the doctors in Maryland and Washington, DC). At times begging for a doctor's appointment through intermediaries and succeeding, sometimes, with a response of "Shhh, don't tell anyone I told you" from a doctor's assistant. Again, my job was easy—just fight this thing as hard as I could. Candy, on the other hand, was facing a grim situation all on her own with no idea of what the future would hold. I had a bevy of doctors and specialists at my side while she had only herself.

People often ask me how all this has changed me. I learned early on that bad things can happen ever since my dad died when I was thirteen. I remember touching his stiff arm in the casket at the wake, then from a distance thinking that he had moved and making my way over to my mother, telling her that this was a mistake and he was still alive. Of course, he was not. So I learned early on that bad things can happen, and I believe that adversity helped me handle the trouble spots of life, even brain cancer and the permanent collateral damage it left behind.

The love and closeness of my family has always been the most important thing in my life and is even more so today. The mutual love, respect, and caring Candy, Kelly, Hadley and I have for each other is what I always dreamed of. So I am living my dream and you can't beat that.

Life is a long road with a lot of potholes, many of which you can't see coming. So I appreciate every day and that I am still here, even if in a lessened state. I am one of the lucky ones, and I hope you are too.

Post Script

As I am just about to finish this book, I was shocked to realize I have been dealt another blow. I woke up in the morning about a week ago due to nudges from my wife. The super loud, annoying buzzing sound from my alarm was having no affect on me. I could not hear a thing!

I made an emergency visit to my Otolaryngologist. The result is that I on a fast track to having an operation to have a Cochlear implant. This means getting a metal plate screwed onto my head and numerous electrodes inserted into my ear. In the meantime, my audiology technician has dialed up my high tech hearing aids to maximum volume.

My wife and I were scheduled for dinner with a group of friends the next evening. I was a hesitant to go, given my recent hearing debacle, but Candy and I figured most of them knew my hearing is impaired so it should be ok—they would not notice that it was any worse than before. Well, it was a lot worse. I tried to fake it the best I could but I was feeling really out of it. Candy had politely tapped my knee a couple of times. Apparently I had been yelling in an attempt to participate in the conversation (I could not hear myself talk).

So, midway thru I decided to take a risk. There was a lot of engaging conversation going on, and I took out a pen and wrote on a napkin "if you are talking about anything interesting could you please provide a brief synopsis below" and I passed it to the person on my right. The first response was straight forward—they were talking about iPad vs Amazon tablet. Then as it was passed around, written by the others at the table came various lascivious remarks. We were all laughing hysterically. More normal notes were passed around as necessary during the evening. I ended up having a wonderful evening. You just never know. I am ready to take on whatever comes next in this seemingly unending journey.

Acknowledgments

There are so many people I would like to thank. I was helped not just by neuro-oncologists, radiation oncologists, pathologists, and brain surgeons but also by nurses, assistants, rehabilitation professionals, and more. I am not able to name them all. So I am listing the ones I can, alphabetically, as follows:

Dr. Tracy Batchelor

Executive Director, Steven E. and Catherine Pappas Center for Neuro-Oncology

Director, Division of Neuro-Oncology

Department of Neuro-Neurology

Professor of Neurology, Harvard Medical School

Peter Black, MD, PhD, FACS

Franc D. Ingraham Professor of Neurosurgery at the Harvard Medical School

Chair of the Department of Neurosurgery at Brigham and Woman's Hospital and at Children's Hospital Boston

Chief of Neurosurgical Oncology at the Dana Farber Cancer

Dr. E. Antonio Chiocca, MD, PhD, FAANS

Chairman, Department of Neurosurgery

Codirector, Institute for the Neurosciences at the Brigham

Brigham and Women's/Faulkner Hospital

Surgical Director, Center for Neuro-Oncology Dana-Farber
Cancer Institute, 75 Francis Street, Boston, MA 02116

Dr. John Coen

Neuro Oncologist at Johns Hopkins Hospital

Dr. Howard Fine, MD

Chief of the Branch of Neuro-Oncology

National Cancer Institute

Former Director of Neuro-Oncology Disease Center

Dr. Jay Loeffler, MD

Chief of Radiation Oncology

Massachusetts Hospital

Michele Lucas, MSW, LICSW

Massachusetts General Hospital Cancer Center

Konrad Mark, MD

Neurologist

Affiliated with Beverly Hospital

Roger J. Packer, MD

Children's National Medical Center

Senior Vice President, Center for Neuroscience and Behavior Medicine

Director, Brain Tumor Institute

Director, Daniel and Jennifer Gilbert Neurofibromatosis

Professor, Neurology and Pediatrics George Washington University

School of Health Sciences

And a special thank-you to Twig Mowatt, who provided technical and literary advice as well as motivation.

The support and outpour of good wishes and encouragement from the North Shore community was unbelievable, uplifting, and helped me stay positive. I heard from friends and friends whom I never knew where friends.

Some of particular note were Jim Deveny, Charlie Sarkis, Maida Broudo, and Bill Dore with his homemade chocolate ice box cakes.

My golfing pals, especially Bob Berg, who never stopped dishing it out. "Raybo, we were shorting you last year"—the investment term for betting on the severe decline in value of something. And my good friend Bob Scriven, who said to me, "I am sure I can find a way to take advantage of your extreme misfortune." You've got to love it!

Background

I grew up in Boxford, Massachusetts, which is about twenty miles north and a little west of Boston. I had three sisters (two older and one younger). Before she married my father, my mother was the assistant to the editor of the *Ladies' Home Journal.* My father had been an all-American in football at West Point and captain of the basketball team in 1932 before he became a war hero. As a colonel in the army air force, he flew multiple fighter missions in the European theater with the famed 365th Hell Hawk squadron of the P47 Thunderbolt unit. He survived a crash and pulled his copilot out of the burning plane to safety. He later retired as a brigadier general before establishing his leather business in Salem, Massachusetts. He died of a heart attack in 1967 shortly after my thirteenth birthday. He was buried at West Point with a twenty-one gun salute. A jet squadron flew overhead with one plane bowing out signifying his loss. The American flag was folded in the traditional ceremonious manner and handed to me, his only son. It is worth noting that his entrance to West Point (as the second alternate) hinged on the fact that the two men appointed ahead of him by district congressman John J. Casey failed the entrance exam. My dad had passed and was admitted—a dream come true for him. At graduation, he was awarded the West Point Saber, given to the best scholar athlete of that year. My father had come a long way from the blue-collar town he grew up in Hazleton, Pennsylvania.

I like to think that whatever determination and courage I have, I inherited from him.

I cannot say that my athletic career was as storied as his, but I played three varsity sports while a senior at Phillips Academy (in Andover, Massachusetts) and blossomed at Union College playing four different varsity sports, eventually settling on lacrosse. I was elected co captain, was the leading scorer on the team and tied for the fourth leading scorer in the country for division II and III, and was awarded the MVP trophy in 1978.

Made in the USA
Lexington, KY
18 November 2012